Cambridge Elements ≡

Elements in Organization Theory
edited by
Nelson Phillips
Imperial College London
Royston Greenwood
University of Alberta

T0311868

HEALTHCARE RESEARCH AND ORGANIZATION THEORY

Trish Reay

University of Alberta

Elizabeth Goodrick

Florida Atlantic University

Thomas D'Aunno

New York University

CAMBRIDGE
UNIVERSITY PRESS

CAMBRIDGE
UNIVERSITY PRESS

University Printing House, Cambridge CB2 8BS, United Kingdom

One Liberty Plaza, 20th Floor, New York, NY 10006, USA

477 Williamstown Road, Port Melbourne, VIC 3207, Australia

314–321, 3rd Floor, Plot 3, Splendor Forum, Jasola District Centre, New Delhi – 110025, India

79 Anson Road, #06–04/06, Singapore 079906

Cambridge University Press is part of the University of Cambridge.

It furthers the University's mission by disseminating knowledge in the pursuit of education, learning, and research at the highest international levels of excellence.

www.cambridge.org
Information on this title: www.cambridge.org/9781009005180
DOI: 10.1017/9781009036375

© Trish Reay, Elizabeth Goodrick, and Thomas D'Aunno 2021

First published 2021

A catalogue record for this publication is available from the British Library.

ISBN 978-1-009-00518-0 Paperback
ISSN 2397-947X (online)
ISSN 2514-3859 (print)

Healthcare Research and Organization Theory

Elements in Organization Theory

DOI: 10.1017/9781009036375
First published online: June 2021

Trish Reay
University of Alberta

Elizabeth Goodrick
Florida Atlantic University

Thomas D'Aunno
New York University

Author for correspondence: Trish Reay, trish.reay@ualberta.ca
Elizabeth Goodrick, goodrick@fau.edu
Thomas D'Aunno, tda3@nyu.edu

Abstract: In this Element, we examine how organizational researchers have published articles contributing to organization theory in high-quality organizational journals, and we examine how healthcare researchers have drawn on organization theory in healthcare management journals. We have two main aims in writing this Element. The first is to motivate scholars working in the field of general organizational and management studies to increasingly use healthcare settings as an empirical context for their work in theory development. Our second aim is to encourage healthcare researchers to increase their use of organizational theory to advance knowledge about the provision of healthcare services. Our investigations revealed a growing number of organizational studies situated in healthcare. We also found a disappointing level of connection between research published in organization journals and research published in healthcare journals. We provide explanations for this division, and encourage more cross-disciplinary work in the future.

Keywords: organization theory, healthcare research, institutional theory, professions, organizational change

ISBNs:9781009005180 (PB), 9781009036375 (OC)
ISSNs:2397-947X (online), 2514-3859 (print)

Contents

1 Introduction to Healthcare Research and Organization
Theory   1

2 How Researchers Use Healthcare Empirical Settings to
Develop Organization Theory   4

3 How Healthcare Studies Use Organization Theory   41

4 Conclusions and Future Research Opportunities   52

References   69

1 Introduction to Healthcare Research and Organization Theory

As organizational scholars who conduct research in healthcare settings, we have often been asked to explain the value of developing organization theory based on studies of hospitals, physicians, or other healthcare professionals when they are so "different" from other organizations and other ways of organizing. In short, we answer by saying it is exactly because healthcare organizations are so highly institutionalized, and so strongly based on a professional workforce, and so tightly connected to government policy that they serve as excellent settings for developing concepts about (for example) organizational change, networks, the diffusion of innovation, resource dependency, social identity, the professions, and institutional theory.

In particular, when qualitative researchers seek contexts that can be classified as "extreme cases," there is an abundance of opportunities in healthcare settings. And as researchers continue the quest to understand whole systems that inherently connect what could be called micro, meso, and macro levels of analysis, healthcare stands out as an ideal setting for empirical investigations. All of this is to say that we have written this Element with the underlying belief that more attention to the value of healthcare settings in the development of organization theory is long overdue.

Thus, we have two overall aims in writing this Element. The first is to motivate scholars working in the field of general organizational and management studies to use the healthcare industry as an empirical context for their work in theory development. Similarly, we aim to encourage those who have already been studying the healthcare industry to use this setting to extend what we know about general management and organization theory. To support this aim, we show the ways that scholars have already developed organization theory through the study of healthcare settings. Indeed, it turns out that, although there has been some variation, the number of articles of this type published in highly ranked theory development journals in the last decade has generally increased over time. In Section 2 we summarize the results from these studies, focusing on the particular contributions they make to theory development.

Our second aim is to encourage healthcare researchers to increase their use of organization theory to advance knowledge about the provision of healthcare services. Kurt Lewin (1951), one of the most prominent social psychologists of his generation, captured our argument well in his dictum, "There is nothing so practical as a good theory." This stands in contrast to our investigation of the citation records of the organization theory articles we identify in Section 2. We found that very few of these articles are referenced in key healthcare journals. We argue that theory-informed healthcare research can produce important insights for managers, policy-makers, and clinicians that they otherwise would have overlooked. To accomplish this aim, in Section 3 we discuss examples of how healthcare management researchers have used organization theory to develop more practical knowledge with the potential to improve access to, and the cost and quality of, healthcare services.

1.1 Why Healthcare?

Throughout the world, healthcare is one of the most passionately and publicly debated aspects of everyday life. Its impact is not only personal but societal and economic as well. Almost all national governments devote time, energy, and resources to developing policy related to healthcare. In terms of economic impact, healthcare spending ranges from approximately 8 percent to more than 16 percent of gross domestic product (GDP), making it one of the largest industries globally. In developing countries, the need for healthcare has a major impact on what can and cannot be accomplished. Common to nearly all countries is the fact that the healthcare needs of many of its citizens are at best only partially met.

Broadly defined, the healthcare industry involves an enormously diverse range of people, technologies, professions, and organizational arrangements, encompassing many types of public, nonprofit, and for-profit organizations. The size, diversity, interconnectedness, complexity, and broad impact of the healthcare sector make it a rich and important setting for conducting organizational and management research.

Although there has been a great deal of research on healthcare, most of this work has focused either on clinical issues or on healthcare policy. These areas have largely been within the domains of scholars in the biological sciences, or in the case of policy, economists and political scientists. In the past few decades, researchers have paid increased attention to studying healthcare organization and management. This shift in focus is entirely appropriate and much needed, in view of the fact that the vast majority of healthcare services are delivered through organizations, whether these are health clinics, hospitals, private practice groups, nursing homes, or laboratories.

Unfortunately, most of the research conducted on healthcare organizations has been published in journals and books that are directed primarily to a healthcare audience. Some of this work draws on the theory and research published in the various disciplines of management (which we discuss in Section 3), although most often it has not. In addition, and also unfortunately, general organizational scholars tend to read or use very little of this work to help inform their research.

As a result, what we know as organizational scholars about the people and organizations providing healthcare has tended to be underdeveloped theoretically. In addition, and perhaps of even greater concern, organizational researchers have typically not looked to the healthcare industry as a forum for testing their theories, thus limiting what can be said about the generalizability of their work outside of traditional business settings. When healthcare settings have been used in studies published in general organizational journals, the distinctive aspects of the healthcare setting are minimized. Although some organizational journals and reviewers for these journals may encourage minimal attention to the research context, we suggest that there are potential advantages to more clearly elaborating the distinctive features of healthcare settings.

1.2 Why Healthcare Is an Excellent Research Setting to Advance Organization Theory

We argue that, compared to other industries, fields, and organizations, healthcare settings provide exceptionally rich contexts for the development of organization theory because:

- Healthcare systems inherently combine macro, meso, and micro levels, facilitating cross-level analyses and whole-system analyses.
- The multilevel interdependencies among frontline workers (especially professionals) and between organizational and field-level actors facilitate research that advance theory about inter- and intraorganizational dynamics, including agency at multiple levels of analysis.
- Diverse professional groups are influential in work arrangements and organizations, giving opportunities for in-depth studies of power and influence as well as the relationships among professions.
- Advanced technologies play a critical role – ranging from genomic work to radiologic imaging, to vaccines and information technology, opening up potential for studying the impact of robotics and blockchain modeling, for example.
- The interplay between relatively tight and complex regulation coupled with demands for professional autonomy is clearly evident in many aspects of service delivery, allowing research that examines conflict and coordination within and across organizational boundaries.
- The intersection of public and private ownership and funding creates opportunities to study how different forms of governance influence organizations and organizational systems.
- The deep ethical and humanitarian concerns that accompany everyday work, especially – but certainly not only – in the midst of deadly pandemics, facilitate attention to the role of emotions and human-centered work.

- The ongoing need for adaptation, structural change, and performance improvement and, at the same time, stability at the organizational and field levels allows researchers to tackle questions regarding change and stability.
- Despite differences between nations and world regions, similarities that exist across the globe in the organization of healthcare systems and organizations facilitate learning at a global level and can help to improve our understanding of the overall complexity of organizations and fields.

In the next sections of this Element, we elaborate these topics. In Section 2 we explain the results of our review of papers published in organizational journals over the last decade. Overall, we show how researchers have used empirical findings from investigations in healthcare settings to advance organization theory. In particular, we highlight contributions to the literature on institutional theory, the professions, social identity, networks, the diffusion of innovation, and organizational change.

In Section 3, we switch our focus to papers published in scholarly healthcare journals, where we examine how healthcare researchers have used organization theory to develop practical knowledge with the potential to improve access to, and the cost and quality of, healthcare services. This review reveals a surprising level of disconnect between research published in organization theory journals and that published in healthcare journals. We show the gap between organization theory articles identified in Section 2 and their use in healthcare articles, and explain how more integrated use of theory could improve healthcare research.

In Section 4, we conclude by presenting our overall views about the need for much tighter connections between organization theory and healthcare research. We also offer suggestions for future research. Since we believe strongly in the value of theory, we argue that healthcare research can be improved with more active use of recent developments in organization theory; we also call on organizational theorists to be more attuned to the results of healthcare research. We contend that theory must be continuously renewed, and that such renewal can only happen when theorists pay attention to empirical confirmation or rebuttal of theory in the context of practice. In the next sections we develop these ideas more fully.

2 How Researchers Use Healthcare Empirical Settings to Develop Organization Theory

In this section we discuss how researchers have contributed to organization theory through the analysis of empirical data from healthcare settings. We see this as an important and interesting question because of our personal engagement as researchers with the rich and multilevel context that healthcare provides, as well as our knowledge of other research in healthcare settings generating thoughtful and novel contributions to different aspects of organization theory. Based on our sense that there are a lot more healthcare articles than there used to be in the top organizational journals, we set out to confirm (or not) our hunches.

Thus, we conducted a systematic search of all articles published from 2009 to 2020 in the following journals: *Academy of Management Journal*, *Administrative Science Quarterly*, *Organization Science*, *Journal of Management Studies*, and *Organization Studies*. We chose these journals because they are focused on publishing manuscripts that make a strong contribution to theory, and collectively they provide academic, geographic, and empirical diversity.

From this set, we identified articles based on empirical research in healthcare settings that contributed to any aspect of organization theory. We excluded articles with a purely microlevel focus, such as worker motivation or participation in teams. We identified seventy-five articles over the almost twelve years of our timeframe, with a peak number of twelve articles published in 2016. (Figure 1 shows the distribution of articles per year.) We then analyzed each of the articles, categorizing them according to their main theoretical contribution. Table 1, which shows our list of articles, provides the foundation for our discussion about the ways in which research conducted in healthcare settings has developed organization theory.

Since we were interested in how healthcare articles make contributions to organization theory, we grouped the articles in our dataset according to the

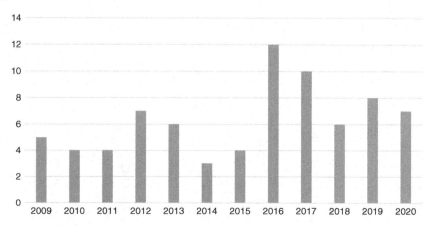

Figure 1 Healthcare-based publications per year
(*note: 2020 is for eight months)

Table 1 Dataset articles categorized by theoretical contribution

Author	Year	Article Title	Journal
		INSTITUTIONAL THEORY	
Institutional Change			
Battilana [total cites = 184 *HC cites = 1]	2011	The Enabling Role of Social Position in Diverging from the Institutional Status Quo: Evidence from the UK National Health Service	*Organization Science*
De Bree & Stoopendaal	2018	De- and Recoupling and Public Regulation	*Organization Studies*
• Finn et al. • [total cites = 85 • *HC cites = 3]	2010	Team Work in Context: Institutional Mediation in the Public-Service Professional Bureaucracy	*Organization Studies*
Hesse et al.	2016	Selective Regulator Decoupling and Organizations' Strategic Responses	*Academy of Management Journal*
• Kellogg • [total cites = 142 • *HC cites = 0]	2011	Hot Lights and Cold Steel: Cultural and Political Toolkits for Practice Change in Surgery	*Organization Science*
• Kellogg • [total cites = 77 • *HC cites = 0]	2012	Making the Cut: Using Status-Based Countertactics to Block Social Movement Implementation and Microinstitutional Change in Surgery	*Organization Science*
Kern et al.	2017	Constructing and Sustaining Counter-institutional Identities	*Organization Studies*

Institutional Logics

Cappellaro et al.	2020	From Logic Acceptance to Logic Rejection: The Process of Destabilization in Hybrid Organizations	*Organization Science*
• Currie & Spyridonidis • [total cites = 134] • *HC cites = 0]	2015	Interpretation of Multiple Institutional Logics on the Ground: Actors' Position, Their Agency and Situational Constraints in Professionalized Contexts	*Organization Studies*
Heinze & Weber	2016	Toward Organizational Pluralism: Institutional Intrapreneurship in Integrative Medicine	*Organization Science*
Martin et al.	2016	Institutional Complexity and Individual Responses: Delineating the Boundaries of Partial Autonomy	*Organization Studies*
• Nigam & Ocasio • [total cites = 384] • *HC cites = 1]	2010	Event Attention, Environmental Sensemaking, and Change in Institutional Logics: An Inductive Analysis of the Effects of Public Attention to Clinton's Health Care Reform Initiative	*Organization Science*
• Pahnke et al. • [total cites = 171] • *HC cites = 0]	2015	Who Takes You to the Dance? How Partners' Institutional Logics Influence Innovation in Young Firms	*Academy of Management Journal*
• Reay & Hinings • [total cites = 1630] • *HC cites = 6]	2009	Managing the Rivalry of Competing Institutional Logics	*Organization Studies*
Reay et al.	2017	Getting Leopards to Change Their Spots: Co-creating a New Professional Role Identity	*Academy of Management Journal*

Table 1 (cont.)

Author	Year	Article Title	Journal
Villani et al.	2017	Understanding Value Creation in Public-Private Partnerships: A Comparative Case Study	*Journal of Management Studies*
Institutional Work			
Goodrick et al.	2020	Preserving a Professional Institution: Emotion in Discursive Institutional Work	*Journal of Management Studies*
Herepath & Kitchener	2016	When Small Bandages Fail: The Field-Level Repair of Severe and Protracted Institutional Breaches	*Organization Studies*
Lawrence	2017	High-Stakes Institutional Translation: Establishing North America's First Government-Sanctioned Supervised Injection Site	*Administrative Science Quarterly*
Nigam & Dokko	2019	Career Resourcing and the Process of Professional Emergence	*Academy of Management Journal*
• Singh & Jayanti • [total cites = 39] • *HC cites = 0]	2013	When Institutional Work Backfires: Organizational Control of Professional Work in the Pharmaceutical Industry	*Academy of Management Journal*
Wright et al.	2017	Maintaining the Values of a Profession: Institutional Work and Moral Emotions in the Emergency Department	*Academy of Management Journal*

PROFESSIONS AND ORGANIZATIONS

	Year	Title	Journal
• Adler & Kwon • [total cites = 109] • *HC cites = 1]	2013	The Mutation of Professionalism as a Contested Diffusion Process: Clinical Guidelines as Carriers of Institutional Change in Medicine	Journal of Management Studies
• Barrett et al. • [total cites = 228] • *HC cites = 6]	2012	Reconfiguring Boundary Relations: Robotic Innovations in Pharmacy Work	Organization Science
Beane	2019	Shadow Learning: Building Robotic Surgical Skill When Approved Means Fail	Administrative Science Quarterly
Bucher et al.	2016	Contestation about Collaboration: Discursive Boundary Work among Professions	Organization Studies
Chown	2020	Financial Incentives and Professionals' Work Tasks: The Moderating Effects of Jurisdictional Dominance and Prominence	Organization Science
• Currie et al. • [total cites = 383] • *HC cites = 9]	2012	Institutional Work to Maintain Professional Power: Recreating the Model of Medical Professionalism	Organization Studies
Galperin	2020	Organizational Powers: Contested Innovation and Loss of Professional Jurisdiction in the Case of Retail Medicine	Organization Science
Kellogg	2019	Subordinate Activation Tactics: Semi-Professionals and Micro-Level Institutional Change in Professional Organizations	Administrative Science Quarterly

Table 1 (cont.)

Author	Year	Article Title	Journal
• McCann et al. • [total cites = 127 • *HC cites = 0]	2013	Still Blue-Collar After All These Years? An Ethnography of the Professionalization of Emergency Ambulance Work	*Journal of Management Studies*
Visser et al.	2018	Unequal Consumers: Consumerist Healthcare Technologies and Their Creation of New Inequalities	*Organization Studies*
Visser et al.	2018	Prying Eyes: A Dramaturgical Approach to Professional Surveillance	*Journal of Management Studies*
Wang et al.	2020	From Grace to Violence: Stigmatizing the Medical Profession in China	*Academy of Management Journal*
• Waring & Currie • [total cites = 384 • *HC cites = 17]	2009	Managing Expert Knowledge: Organizational Challenges and Managerial Futures for the UK Medical Profession	*Organization Studies*
Wilhelm et al.	2020	White Coats at the Coalface: The Standardizing Work of Professions at the Frontline	*Organization Studies*
		SOCIAL IDENTITY THEORY	
Chreim et al.	2020	Constructing and Sustaining Counter-Institutional Identities	*Academy of Management Journal*

Author	Year	Title	Journal
Croft et al. [total cites = 68] *HC cites = 1]	2015	The Impact of Emotionally Important Social Identities on the Construction of a Managerial Leader Identity: A Challenge for Nurses in the English National Health Service	Organization Studies
Currie et al. [total cites = 145] *HC cites = 4]	2010	Role Transition and the Interaction of Relational and Social Identity: New Nursing Roles in the English NHS	Organization Studies
De Rond & Lok	2016	Some Things Can Never Be Unseen: The Role of Context in Psychological Injury at War	Academy of Management Journal
DiBenigno	2018	Anchored Personalization in Managing Goal Conflict between Professional Groups: The Case of U.S. Army Mental Health Care	Administrative Science Quarterly
DiBenigno & Kellogg [total cites = 79] *HC cites = 0]	2014	Beyond Occupational Differences: The Importance of Cross-Cutting Demographics and Dyadic Toolkits for Collaboration in a U.S. Hospital	Administrative Science Quarterly
Goodrick & Reay [total cites = 169] *HC cites = 3]	2010	Florence Nightingale Endures: Legitimizing a New Professional Role Identity	Journal of Management Studies
Kryatsis et al.	2017	Health Systems in Transition: Professional Identity Work in the Context of Shifting Institutional Logics	Academy of Management Journal

Table 1 (cont.)

Author	Year	Article Title	Journal
		NETWORK THEORY	
• Battilana & Casciaro • [total cites = 485] • *HC cites = 1]	2012	Change Agents, Networks, and Institutions: A Contingency Theory of Organizational Change	*Academy of Management Journal*
• Currie & White • [total cites = 192] • *HC cites = 7]	2012	Inter-Professional Barriers and Knowledge Brokering in an Organizational Context: The Case of Healthcare	*Organization Studies*
D'Andreta et al.	2016	Dominant Cognitive Frames and the Innovative Power of Social Networks	*Organization Studies*
• Tasselli • [total cites = 70] • *HC cites = 2]	2015	Social Networks and Inter-Professional Knowledge Transfer: The Case of Healthcare Professionals	*Organization Studies*
		DIFFUSION OF INNOVATION	
• Compagni et al. • [total cites = 103] • *HC cites = 2]	2014	How Early Implementations Influence Later Adoptions of Innovation: Social Positioning and Skill Reproduction in the Diffusion of Robotic Surgery	*Academy of Management Journal*
Gardner et al.	2017	Achieving Time-Sensitive Organizational Performance Through Mindful Use of Technologies and Routines	*Organization Science*
Greenwood et al.	2019	The Role of Individual and Organizational Expertise in the Adoption of New Practices	*Organization Science*

Author	Year	Title	Journal
Gupta & Khanna	2019	A Recombination-Based Internationalization Model: Evidence from Narayana Health's Journey from India to the Cayman Islands	Organization Science
Kennedy & Fiss • [total cites = 572] • *HC cites = 1]	2009	Institutionalization, Framing, and Diffusion: The Logic of TQM Adoption and Implementation Decisions Among U.S. Hospitals	Academy of Management Journal
Nigam et al.	2016	Explaining the Selection of Routines for Change during Organizational Search	Administrative Science Quarterly
Polidoro & Theeke • [total cites = 60] • *HC cites = 0]	2012	Getting Competition Down to a Science: The Effects of Technological Competition on Firms' Scientific Publications	Organization Science
Reay et al. • [total cites = 106] • *HC cites = 2]	2013	Transforming New Ideas into Practice: An Activity Based Perspective on the Institutionalization of Practices	Journal of Management Studies
Roopa & Bharadwaj • [total cites = 22] • *HC cites = 0]	2012	Power Differentials and Performative Deviation Paths in Practice Transfer: The Case of Evidence-Based Medicine	Organization Science
Vakili & McGahan	2016	Health Care's Grand Challenge: Stimulating Basic Science on Diseases That Primarily Afflict the Poor	Academy of Management Journal
Van Grinsven et al.	2020	Identities in Translation: Management Concepts as Means and Outcomes of Identity Work	Organization Studies

Table 1 (cont.)

Author	Year	Article Title	Journal
• Wilkesmann et al. • [total cites = 95] • *HC cites = 0]	2009	The Absence of Cooperation Is Not Necessarily Defection: Structural and Motivational Constraints of Knowledge Transfer in a Social Dilemma Situation	*Organization Studies*
		ORGANIZATIONAL CHANGE	
Antino et al.	2019	Structuring Reality Through the Faultlines Lens: The Effects of Structure, Fairness, and Status Conflict on the Activated Faultlines–Performance Relationship	*Academy of Management Journal*
Aristidou & Barrett	2018	Coordinating Service Provision in Dynamic Service Settings: A Position-Practice Relations Perspective	*Academy of Management Journal*
Caldwell et al.	2017	Social Value Creation and Relational Coordination in Public-Private Collaborations	*Journal of Management Studies*
Christianson	2019	More and Less Effective Updating: The Role of Trajectory Management in Making Sense Again	*Administrative Science Quarterly*
• Clark et al. • [total cites = 41] • *HC cites = 0]	2013	Learning from Customers: Individual and Organizational Effects in Outsourced Radiological Services	*Organization Science*
Dattée & Barlow	2017	Multilevel Organizational Adaptation: Scale Invariance in the Scottish Healthcare System	*Organization Science*

Author	Year	Title	Journal
Desai	2020	Can Busy Organizations Learn to Get Better? Distinguishing Between the Competing Effects of Constrained Capacity on the Organizational Learning Process	Organization Science
• Desai • [total cites = 67 • *HC cites = 0]	2014	Learning Through the Distribution of Failures within an Organization: Evidence from Heart Bypass Surgery Performance	Academy of Management Journal
Dupret	2018	Performative Silences: Potentiality of Organizational Change	Organization Studies
Gardner et al.	2017	Achieving Time-Sensitive Organizational Performance Through Mindful Use of Technologies and Routines	Organization Science
Heaphy	2017	"Dancing on Hot Coals": How Emotion Work Facilitates Collective Sensemaking	Academy of Management Journal
• King et al. • [total cites = 131 • *HC cites = 1]	2011	Why Organizational and Community Diversity Matter: Representativeness and the Emergence of Incivility and Organizational Performance	Academy of Management Journal
Kislov et al.	2017	New Game, Old Rules? Mechanisms and Consequences of Legitimation in Boundary Spanning Activities	Organization Studies
• Lockett et al. • [total cites = 126 • *HC cites = 0]	2014	The Influence of Social Position on Sensemaking about Organizational Change	Academy of Management Journal

Table 1 (cont.)

Author	Year	Article Title	Journal
Maltarich et al.	2017	Pay-for-Performance, Sometimes: An Interdisciplinary Approach to Integrating Economic Rationality with Psychological Emotion to Predict Individual Performance	*Academy of Management Journal*
McGivern et al.	2017	The Silent Politics of Temporal Work: A Case Study of a Management Consultancy Project to Redesign Public Health Care	*Organization Studies*
• Nembhard & Tucker • [total cites = 123] • *HC cites = 7]	2011	Deliberate Learning to Improve Performance in Dynamic Service Settings: Evidence from Hospital Intensive Care Units	*Organization Science*
Pine & Mazmanian	2016	Artful and Contorted Coordinating: The Ramifications of Imposing Formal Logics of Task Jurisdiction on Situated Practice	*Academy of Management Journal*
• Van Offenbeek et al. • [total cites = 12] • *HC cites = 0]	2009	Enacting Fit in Work Organization and Occupational Structure Design: The Case of Intermediary Occupations in a Dutch Hospital	*Organization Studies*
Wiedner & Mantere	2019	Cutting the Cord: Mutual Respect, Organizational Autonomy, and Independence in Organizational Separation Processes	*Administrative Science Quarterly*

[*HC Journals = *Health Care Management Review; Medical Care Research and Review; Health Services Research; Milbank Quarterly;* and *Social Science and Medicine*] general type of theoretical contributions as set out by the authors. We identified six broad areas: institutional theory (including subcomponents of institutional change, institutional logics, and institutional work); professions and organizations; social identity; networks; diffusion of innovation; and organizational change. In subsections 2.1 to 2.6 we discuss each of these areas in turn, providing background explanations and explaining how the articles in our dataset advance theory by conducting empirical studies in healthcare settings. We note that some published articles make contributions to more than one theory, and in these cases we identify a primary category in Table 1, and also discuss these articles in more than one subsection.

2.1 Institutional Theory

Institutional theory has become a dominant approach in the study of organizations. Broadly explained, institutional theory provides answers to questions about why organizations tend to look the same, how they persist over time, and how they sometimes change (Scott, 2014). As an important part of explaining ongoing stability, scholars developed the concept of "decoupling" – the extent to which organizations could respond to institutional demands by symbolically adopting policies and procedures, but not using them in actual practice (Meyer & Rowan, 1978).

Over the years, there has been significant empirical support for the central arguments of institutional theory (e.g., Heugens & Lander, 2009), and the proportion of published articles in organization journals that include "institution" in the title, the abstract, or the keywords has doubled over less than twenty years (Alvesson & Blom, 2018). As important markers in the timeline of institutional theory, two editions of the SAGE *Handbook of Organizational Institutionalism* (Greenwood et al., 2008, 2017) reenergized and expanded the scope of institutional scholarship by drawing attention to important organizational phenomena through the integration of concepts related to complex institutional environments, power, agency, and practices into institutional thought.

Given these developments, we argue that it is more accurate and useful to conceive of "institutional theory" not as a traditional theory per se with a unified set of propositions, but rather as an umbrella for an important group of related concepts and principles (Kraatz, 2020; Ocasio & Gai, 2020). In subsections 2.1.1 to 2.1.3 we discuss each of the following categories of articles evident in our review of studies based on healthcare settings that contribute to institutional theory: institutional change, institutional logics, and institutional work. We note that the number of articles in this section is relatively large at twenty-one publications. This is not particularly surprising given the ongoing changes in macrolevel system design and associated practice-level alterations – topics that lend themselves well to institutional approaches.

2.1.1 Institutional Change

Although earlier institutional approaches focused on explaining stability (e.g., DiMaggio & Powell, 1983), studies in the past two decades have turned attention to understanding how change can occur in fields and practices that are highly institutionalized. Institutional theory evolved to recognize the importance of processes by which institutions change, with a particular focus on the role that agency among organizations and individuals plays in enabling change (Greenwood et al., 2017; Ocasio & Gai, 2020). Scholars investigating change in healthcare settings have contributed to these advances, building a more dynamic understanding of institutional environments and how they can change.

Healthcare settings illustrate the typical picture of resilient organizational environments (organizational fields) that are characterized by widely held and taken-for-granted societal beliefs and values that are difficult to change. Yet researchers studying healthcare settings have helped to advance theory about institutional change by showing the conditions under which individuals and organizations can engage in reflection about assumptions that underpin their behavior and take action that leads to long-term macrolevel change. For example, in an ethnographic study of hospital units responding to national policy changes, Kellogg (2009) showed the important role that rhetoric, power and politics, and mobilizing support from coworkers could play in changing institutionalized practices. Somewhat similarly, Reay et al. (2006) explained how microlevel actors could engage in purposeful action designed to achieve system-level change. These articles contributed to a significant turning point in the literature on institutional change by drawing attention to microlevel processes that encouraged researchers to further develop theory regarding the potential for intraorganizational dynamics to facilitate (or prevent) institutional change.

In analyzing our dataset of articles that contribute to theory about institutional change through empirical studies of healthcare settings (see Table 1), we identified two groups. First, we discuss papers that focused on understanding how change can occur in practices that are highly institutionalized, and how such practice change is connected with macrolevel institutional change. Second, we examine papers that investigated how decoupling, which was previously associated with institutional stability, can be an important component of institutional change.

Changing institutionalized practices. Healthcare settings are characterized by highly institutionalized sets of practices that align with established principles of providing care. As a result, they provide excellent opportunities for researchers to investigate proposed and actual practice change that occurs within larger initiatives construed as institutional change. For example, building on her ethnographic research in hospitals and primary care clinics, Kellogg (2011, 2012) further developed theory in two related articles by showing how proposed changes in the training of surgery residents led to system-level changes in some cases, but not others. The research revealed both the difficulty in enacting institutional change and the importance of cultural tools (e.g., frames, identities) and political toolkits (e.g., staffing, accountability, and evaluation systems) as critical resources in doing so. The focus on cultural and political tools has been picked up and used more broadly in institutional studies, consistently showing the importance of a repertoire of frontline tactics to accomplish broader institutional change.

Taking a more structural approach, Battilana (2011) also examined factors associated with institutional change in the organizational field of hospitals. She focused particularly on the relationship between the social position of individuals and their organizations and their likelihood of initiating organizational changes that challenged the institutional status quo. The results from analyses of data from ninety-three hospitals and their clinics in the United Kingdom show that individuals from lower-status organizations and lower-status professional or occupational groups – that is, actors on the periphery of organizational fields – were more likely to challenge the status quo. This study thus contributed to theory by showing how the position of individuals in an organizational hierarchy matters: higher-level individuals are more likely to challenge established practices within their organizations, but less likely to do so in the broader healthcare field.

As a final example, Currie, Finn, and Martin (2010) also demonstrated how professional actors took on the role of institutional agents, and thus extended institutional theory by revealing the importance of actor choices and their use of political tools to enact change or maintain stability in a professional institution. Together, these articles show the importance of connections between the practice and organizational or field levels, and the ways in which institutional change can occur.

The dynamics of decoupling. While earlier work showed how decoupling can be a mechanism for institutional stability, articles in our dataset highlight how decoupling can facilitate change. Kern, Laguecir, and Leca (2017) studied differences in the responses of two hospital departments to a new government policy requiring the use of a new patient case-mix system. The results showed that the surgery department "implemented" the policy only rhetorically: surgeons ignored and routinely violated the related rules, and clinical practices remained unchanged. In contrast, physicians in the cardiology department used the decoupling opportunity to make changes in practice that aligned with their own local goals – gaining organizational power as a result. Hesse, Krishnan, and Moers (2016) examined decoupling from the perspective of a regulatory agency, the US Centers for Medicare & Medicaid Services (CMS). They argued that regulatory agencies often face conflicting pressures from a variety of stakeholders, and, in response, they engage in decoupling through selective enforcement of standards. Their results showed that CMS balanced conflicting pressures to be tough on fraud while maintaining community access to essential but unprofitable services, such as charity care and medical education. CMS regulators selectively decoupled and exhibited leniency in enforcement of mispricing practices toward "beneficent hospitals," enabling change in hospital practices that continued over time.

In a final example, de Bree and Stoopendaal (2018) studied decoupling in the Dutch healthcare industry, identifying how public regulators recognized and took action to avoid potentially negative consequences. They showed that by using system-based regulation, the gap between the formal and the actual world could be diminished. Considered collectively, these three studies open up theoretical advancements regarding the possibility of decoupling serving as a source of institutional change as well as an explanation for institutional stability.

2.1.2 Institutional Logics

Institutional logics are organizing principles that guide the behavior of actors within a field (Friedland & Alford, 1991). Early explanations about the importance of institutional logics suggested that each organizational field was guided by a dominant logic, although processes of change over time could result in the creation and eventual dominance of a new logic (Scott, 2014; Scott et al., 2000; Thornton & Ocasio, 1999). The construct of an institutional logic was particularly relevant in understanding change in a healthcare field, as shown by the theoretically important book, *Institutional Change and Healthcare Organizations: From Professional Dominance to Managed Care* (2000), by Richard Scott and coauthors. By conducting a detailed analysis of changes in the provision of healthcare in the San Francisco Bay Area, Scott et al. showed how the organizing principle (guiding logic) transitioned over time from a system guided by the logic of professionalism to new arrangements guided by a logic of managerialism, or managed care. This influential work built on and incorporated many concepts of institutional theory as developed by Scott in editions of his book titled *Institutions and Organizations* (the fourth edition was published in 2014); it also brought to increased prominence the theoretical value of studying healthcare settings. Scott and colleagues (2000) took advantage of the fact that the provision of health services relies on the coordinated action of multiple actors in the field to reveal how these different actors could be guided by different logics and that shifts in the relevant actors could impact the dominant logic for the field.

Many organizational researchers have drawn on Scott's ideas about institutional logics and how they can change over time. Studies situated in healthcare settings have revealed interesting dynamics regarding ways in which coexisting logics can impact organizational behavior. For example, Reay and Hinings (2005) examined changes in a Canadian healthcare system, explaining how battles between key field-level actors can lead to a situation of "uneasy truce." Other research based on a historical study of US pharmacists showed how multiple logics can be rearranged in different constellations over time, providing evolving sets of guiding principles for the organizational field (Goodrick & Reay, 2011). These ideas about institutional logics and the importance of multiple logics in healthcare were previously examined using different terminology by D'Aunno, Sutton, and Price (1991). They studied changes in community mental health centers as they diversified into drug abuse treatment in response to conflicting environmental demands. We highlight these studies to show how changes in guiding principles (institutional logics) that are critically important for healthcare settings can provide excellent opportunities to learn about the dynamics of actor interaction within an organizational field.

In analyzing our dataset of articles published from 2009 to 2020, we note that a number of researchers have continued to advance theory by studying cases where multiple logics coexist in a healthcare field. We categorize these studies as advancing organization theory in two ways. First, some studies situated at a field or organizational level reveal new insights into how different arrangements of logics and the ways in which they are interconnected can lead to field-level changes over time. Second, other studies draw on cases situated in healthcare to show how actors affiliated with specific logics can exercise agency in a quest for change or to sustain the status quo. We explain each of these categories here.

Since the conceptualization of multiple logics coexisting in a field matches well with many healthcare systems around the world, it is really not surprising that many scholars have used this macrolevel setting to improve theory about ways that change in the set of guiding logics occurs. Reay and Hinings (2009) showed how competing logics held by different actors could be sustained over lengthy periods of time, facilitating further research into the ways in which coexisting logics impacted field dynamics, and vice versa. Nigam and Ocasio (2010) studied how events in the United States associated with President Clinton's healthcare reform proposal created opportunities for significant changes in institutional logics guiding the field. They contributed to theory by explaining how the meaning of an existing logic could be dramatically changed through ongoing societal debate. This finding advanced knowledge about institutional logics because it highlighted the potential for actors to change their interpretation of logics, paving the way for further research focusing on sensemaking as an important component of change processes. A recent article by Cappellaro, Tracey, and Greenwood (2020) examined how the introduction of a new logic could initially be well accepted, but then later be firmly rejected by field actors. They studied an Italian hospital that adopted a private logic in contrast to the previous guiding arrangement of hybrid professional and public logics, showing how interactions among the audience, organization, and practice levels can lead to internal tensions that overturn previous "success." All of these studies point to the importance of multiple logics in healthcare settings and show how the combination of logics plays a role in the way services are provided.

At the organizational level, other studies in healthcare settings have advanced theory about the value of engaging with institutional logics in different ways (e.g., Heinze & Weber, 2016; Pahnke, Katila, & Eisenhardt, 2015; Villani, Greco, & Phillips, 2017). Villani et al. (2017) studied Italian public–private partnerships in the healthcare sector to show how different ways of combining existing logics created value for different stakeholders. Somewhat similarly, Pahnke et al. (2015) studied the US surgical device industry and found that different funding partners were guided by different institutional logics, and these differences explained variation in firm approach to the provision of venture capital. Further, Heinze and Weber (2016) showed how actors could integrate a new logic (integrative medicine) into highly institutionalized organizations by using opportunistic tactics that facilitated the alignment of new and existing logics. In all these studies, organizational initiatives provided researchers with rich data about the potential advantages or disadvantages of organizational engagement with particular institutional logics.

A third set of articles used the healthcare setting to investigate how actors could take advantage of multiple coexisting institutional logics. Martin et al. (2016) showed how some healthcare actors could navigate and manipulate the three guiding logics (professional, market, and corporate) in ways that allowed them opportunities to implement desired changes. However, they also showed that other actors in similar situations were unable to take advantages of the three logics, with the result that their agency was constrained. Currie and Spyridonidis (2015) also investigated actors' ability to rearrange and blend together different logics in attempts to facilitate change. They found that the status of different actors was a key factor in achieving success. In addition, Reay et al. (2017) showed how different actors could purposely reinterpret multiple logics and their interrelationships to achieve change in approaches to the provision of primary healthcare. All these studies helped to advance theory about institutional logics by showing the potential for savvy actors to take advantage of gaps or connections among or between different logics as part of initiatives to accomplish desired change.

2.1.3 Institutional Work

Lawrence and Suddaby (2006) introduced the concept of institutional work, defining it as purposive action aimed at creating, maintaining, and disrupting institutions and organizations. These ideas were further developed in an influential edited volume (Lawrence, Suddaby, & Leca, 2009) that inspired a growing body of studies, including many that draw on the field of healthcare for their empirical work. The concept of institutional work builds on ideas put forward by DiMaggio (1988) regarding institutional entrepreneurship, and serves as an important avenue for gaining knowledge about the incorporation of agency into institutional theory.

Somewhat similarly to some of the research on institutional change and institutional logics, studies based on healthcare settings have been able to analyze data from multiple levels of analysis that shows how purposeful actions can maintain, disturb, or restore the status quo. In our dataset, we identified three different ways that scholars contributed to the literature on institutional work through their empirical studies. These are: research investigating the strategic use of rhetoric, managing emotions, and establishing new practices.

Strategic use of rhetoric.   Through their examination of textual materials, Herepath and Kitchener (2016) showed how various kinds of rhetoric (e.g., appeals to emotions vs. appeals to data) could be strategically used as part of institutional work. They developed the concept of institutional repair work to highlight purposeful actions that helped to repair relationships between healthcare providers and patients that were damaged following public reports of patient injuries caused by errors in the English National Health Service (NHS). This study made important contributions to theory by showing how rhetoric is a form of institutional work that can impact the key pillars of institutional fields: regulatory (government bodies), normative (professional associations), and cognitive or "mental models" (Scott, 2014). Goodrick, Jarvis, and Reay (2020) also focused on the use of rhetoric, showing how editorials in the *Journal of the American Pharmacist Association* systematically employed different discrete emotions in specific rhetorical argument structures over the course of an institutional project to preserve the profession of pharmacy. They advanced the literature on institutional work by showing that such discursive techniques can vary over time in response to significant events and changes in practices of the target audience.

Managing emotions.   An important and relatively new focus of research contributing to theory about institutional work is the study of emotions and their role in processes of change. Zietsma et al. (2019) gives a comprehensive overview of this literature. In addition, Lawrence (2017) provided an excellent example of how emotional work helped to promote what he termed "high-stakes institutional translation" – in this instance, the opening of a supervised injection site for users of illegal drugs. Through the analysis of rich ethnographic data that revealed the highly emotional nature of actions, conversations, and policy documents, Lawrence showed the critical importance of strategically using rhetoric to achieve the desired outcomes (opening and sustaining the safe injection site). This study also contributed to theory on institutional work by showing how agentic behavior can be influenced by both negative and positive emotions. Wright, Zammuto, and Liesch (2017) also focused on the role of emotions in accomplishing institutional work. They studied how emergency room physicians drew on their moral emotions as they took actions to sustain their professional roles and values in the face of ongoing workplace problems. This research makes important theoretical contributions by showing the potential for moral emotions to critically impact institutional (maintaining) work. These two studies based on healthcare research have contributed to the creation of a new approach to institutional work that recognizes and incorporates the powerful aspect of emotions.

Establishing new practices.   Two articles in our dataset focus on institutional work by paying particular attention to the level of practice. Nigam and Dokko (2019) studied the development of health services researchers as a new profession. They argued that individuals can create a new profession by engaging in practices to deliberately build a professional community and an infrastructure to support the profession. In addition, they identified particular career actions that can lead to the institutionalization of a new profession and, in doing so, advanced understanding of how new institutions emerge.

In their examination of institutional work, Singh and Jayanti (2013) showed how efforts to control the work of professionals can fail. They studied the actions of managers in the pharmaceutical industry and analyzed their use of scripts to control the behavior of sales professionals in their interactions with physicians. The results from their case study showed that in the context of multiple logics and roles, including those of clients, scripts designed to establish new practice can fail if they are too simple for the complex situations in which they are embedded. These two articles that develop theory about establishing new practice in highly institutionalized environments rely on rich data from healthcare settings where professionals work on the front line. As such, the researchers had opportunities to gain insights into microlevel dynamics of change that can impact (positively or negatively) organizational and policy goals.

Summary.   Articles based on research in healthcare settings have contributed to advancing the literature on institutional change, institutional logics, and institutional work. Regarding institutional change, research showed how practices can change in highly institutionalized settings, and how practice change can be associated with institutional change. Research has also revealed how (contrary to previously established theory) decoupling can be an important component of institutional change. Regarding institutional logics, research has advanced theory in two ways – first, revealing new insights into the arrangement of logics within a field and the associated changes; and second, studies showed how actors affiliated with specific logics can exercise agency as part of a change process. Finally, regarding institutional work, researchers have contributed to theory in three ways. First, studies show how actors can strategically use rhetoric to accomplish desired outcomes. Second, researchers have revealed how emotions can be an important component of institutional work. Third, studies have advanced theory by focusing on ways in which new practices can be established through the purposeful action of institutional agents.

2.2 Professions and Organizations

Healthcare settings are characterized by a highly professionalized workforce, providing an excellent opportunity to examine professions and how they are maintained in organizational environments. Traditionally, the study of professions was considered part of the sociological literature, focusing on how professions develop and change over time (see Muzio et al., 2019 for a comprehensive review). As a prototypical profession, physicians and their role in organizations have been an ongoing focus for researchers. Physicians embody the autonomous peer-oriented practice that was seen as a defining characteristic of classic professions (Freidson, 1970, 2001). Early studies characterized professions as important for society because they provided a moral foundation and sustained social order (e.g., Carr-Saunders & Wilson, 1933; Durkheim, 1957; Parsons, 1951). However, beginning in the late 1960s and 1970s, sociological theory on the professions began to move away from conceptualizing professions as rational goal-oriented systems, instead focusing on explanations that emphasized the social and political power of professional groups. This "conflict perspective" on professions emphasized that professionalism was not an inherent characteristic of particular occupations, but rather the outcome of organizing and controlling an occupation (Muzio, Brock, & Suddaby, 2013). Consistent with this view, scholars proposed that theory should focus on how physicians (or other professionals) engaged in professional projects (Larson, 1977) where they made claims about the nature of their expertise as a way to gain government support for credentialing, thus maximizing their status and financial rewards.

Healthcare professions have continued to be a topic of interest, especially as theory evolved to understand how professions can be part of systems as opposed to working in isolation. Abbott (1988) argued that professions operate as part of interdependent systems where different occupations make claims on similar task domains. As a result, shifts in the occupational domain of one profession impact nearby professions or the creation of new occupations (Reay, Goodrick, & Hinings, 2016). Since the provision of healthcare has increasingly required the engagement of multiple occupations, this setting became a natural research site for a systems approach to the professions. Numerous studies have investigated the shifting disciplinary boundaries among professional groups in healthcare, showing how collaboration or competition over tasks can lead to change (e.g., Feyereisen, Brochek, & Goodrick, 2018; Nancarrow & Borthwick, 2005).

More recently, organizational scholars have become interested in the study of professions. This change reflects a number of societal and intellectual developments. The traditional sociological portrayal of professionals paid little, if any, attention to the role of organizations; however, this attention has increased as professionals increasingly work within large organizations, and with a growth in professions that originate inside organizations. The founding of the *Journal of Professions and Organization* is a marker of this shift.

As well, the dominant conflict perspective on professions tended to downplay the normative aspects that professionals play in social life (Burrage & Torstendahl, 1990), making the topic of interest for organization theory. As part of more societal or field-level approaches, institutional accounts increasingly focused attention on the role of the professions in providing stability, or sometimes change, for a system of organizations (Scott, 2014). By emphasizing both that professions are institutions and that professionals are the preeminent institutional agents of our time (Scott, 2008), this approach renewed interest in the normative aspects of institutions.

In analyzing our dataset of articles published in organizational journals, we found that healthcare research contexts consistently provided fertile ground for the development of theory about professions, professionalization, and professionals. A defining characteristic of this literature is a focus on the myriad ways that organizations can impact professional dynamics. We broadly categorized these articles into those focused on a single profession and those concerned with boundaries between or among multiple professions.

A number of articles build theory by focusing on a single profession and showing how organizations can play a role in challenging some of the core characteristics associated with professionals. Adler and Kwon (2013) investigated how physicians' traditional autonomy was challenged by various economic and organizational forces by focusing on the diffusion of clinical guidelines that rationalized healthcare delivery in hospitals. Building on this, Wilhelm, Bullinger, and Chromik (2020) found that such standardization can be maintained as opposed to resisted by physicians when it provides a solution to a pressing problem such as the lack of organizational resources or inconsistent medical socialization of junior professionals.

While both of these papers focus on challenges to the autonomy traditionally enjoyed by professionals, Wang, Raynard, and Greenwood (2020) documented the loss of the "social trusteeship" dimension of medical professionalism in their study of the stigmatization of Chinese physicians. They showed how physicians responded to the economic incentives of hospitals to generate revenue by oversubscribing prescription drugs so as to maximize their income. Visser et al. (2018) focused on the effects of challenges by consumerism to the traditional role of physicians as arbitrators of expertise and quality. They found that differential assessments of technologies associated with consumerism reinforced inequities among patients. Also considering the impact of changing organizational environments, Beane (2019) showed how traditional ways of professional learning can become inappropriate; surgical residents in robotic surgery had limited opportunity to learn from mentors and thus had to become proficient through alternative processes such as the independent use of simulators, watching video-recorded procedures, and working with minimal supervision.

Other studies focused on changes in the relationship between professionals and organizations. The findings of both Chown (2020) and Kellogg (2018) challenge the traditional idea that professionals are self-governing by explicating tactics that managers can use to influence professionals to change their practices. Chown (2020) showed that physicians, similar to other workers, can be influenced by financial incentives, but the effectiveness of such incentives is related to the characteristics of the tasks in question. She found that the efficacy of financial incentives was dependent on the extent to which the tasks were performed by physicians (as opposed to a different health professional), as well as the extent to which the tasks comprised a high percentage of the physicians' work. Somewhat similarly, Kellogg (2018) investigated how professionals could be influenced to change their practices, focusing on the role of semiprofessionals rather than financial incentives. She showed how the favorable structural position of subordinate semiprofessionals vis-à-vis physicians can be used to accomplish change on the manager's behalf. Collectively, these studies suggest that professional control over members and organizations is weakening over time as organizational managers learn more effective ways to control professional behavior.

A second theme in our papers focusing on a single profession is that professions at the field level are interwoven with their enactment at the organizational level. For example, McCann et al. (2013) focused on the professional project of emergency ambulance work. They showed that policy changes in the UK's NHS resulted in the development of field-level structural trappings of a profession (e.g., training and certification in institutions of higher education, research journals, codes of practices, and a professional association), but the actual work of paramedics did not correspondingly change. This study highlights how organizational control over the practice of paramedics resulted in their everyday work reproducing their blue-collar professionalism rather than changing it.

The set of papers focused on multiple professionals explored relationships among different professionals and how they maintained or changed their practice domains. These studies developed theory by building on Abbott's (1988) conception of professionals as part of a system characterized by jurisdictional competition between occupational groups with similar or overlapping task domains. The healthcare context in each case provided an excellent setting for exploring boundary issues because of the numerous professionals working in a given domain with clearly demarcated status differences.

Drawing on the idea of boundary work, Gieryn (1983, 1999) and Bucher et al. (2016) showed how five professional health associations discursively responded to a government proposal to strengthen interprofessional collaboration. They contribute to the literature by showing how, in situations of contested boundaries, the field-level status and centrality of professional groups influence the choice of framing strategy.

Also focused on interprofessional dynamics, Currie et al. (2012) linked the professions literature with that on institutional work (Lawrence & Suddaby, 2006) to show how professionals can engage in activities that maintain or change prevailing institutional arrangements. Studying how specialist physicians (clinical geneticists) responded to organizational attempts to replace them with general practitioners or nurses, Currie et al. (2012) showed how institutional work by professionals could effectively associate the concept of risk with changes in service delivery to maintain the model of medical professionalism.

Barrett et al. (2012) studied intraprofessional behavior, showing how the introduction of robots prompted the reorganization of the activities of three interdependent occupational groups involved in pharmacy work. This study revealed how a technological disruption can alter occupational boundaries, resulting in the expansion of roles for both parties. Visser et al. (2018) studied microlevel interactions to explore how healthcare professionals responded to the introduction of surveillance technology that threatened their traditional autonomy. They creatively found ways to use the technology to display their expertise and modify disciplinary boundaries. These two studies contribute to our understanding of how technology can be involved in the reworking of disciplinary boundaries. Finally, Galperin (2020) showed how nonprofessional market actors, specifically corporations, can capitalize on longstanding jurisdictional tensions. This study revealed how physician control over medical work was weakened through the introduction of retail medicine shops where nurse practitioners' jurisdictional claims were elevated in comparison to those of physicians. Collectively, this large number of articles investigating the dynamics between different healthcare professions substantially advances theory about boundary work and the interface between professions and organizations.

Summary.   Articles based on healthcare settings contribute to theory about professions and organizations in two ways. First, by focusing on a single profession, they reveal new understandings of how professions can grow stronger or weaker and how new professions can emerge. Second, by analyzing multiple groupings of healthcare professionals, studies have improved our knowledge base regarding boundary work among professions and how conflict or collaboration can impact processes of change.

2.3 Social Identity

Organizational researchers have developed and sustained a strong interest in the concept of identity. Identity is a sense of self that answers the question "who am I?" or "who are we?" and has implications for how people act. The concept of social identity was introduced to the organizational literature by Ashforth and Mael (1989), and since then has been used at multiple analytical levels including individual, group, and organizational. Social identity refers to the ways in which people's self-concepts are based on their membership in groups, including religions, nationalities, occupations, social class, and organizations. Thus, definitions of self are relational because they are derived through intergroup comparisons and enacted in relation to others (Stryker, 2007; Tajfel & Turner, 1985).

Healthcare contexts provide particularly rich opportunities to study professional identity because of the highly professionalized nature of the work. A number of studies advance theory by tailoring an identity frame to improve our understanding of professionals. Professional identity is critical to theory about professional roles and behavior since professionals develop intense connections to their work through lengthy educational and socialization processes. In their groundbreaking study of medical residents, Pratt, Rockmann, and Kaufmann (2006) showed how professionals developed their identity in close connection with the work they did rather than the organizations in which they were embedded. This approach built on earlier research that emphasized the importance of roles and role enactment as central aspects of identity (Stryker & Serpe, 1982), and led to further research revealing the particularly strong link between roles and identity for professionals (e.g., Chreim, Williams, & Hinings, 2007). With ongoing interest in how identity can change over time, the concept of identity work (how identity is constructed, maintained, or revised) became another key concept of interest in studies of organizations generally, and healthcare organizations specifically (Alvesson, Lee Ashcraft, & Thomas, 2008; Alvesson & Willmott, 2002; Schwalbe & Mason-Schrock, 1996).

In the studies we reviewed, we found that healthcare contexts were used as rich data sources to develop new theory about processes of identity change in response to shifts in the environment. Goodrick and Reay (2010) explained how a new professional role identity could be discursively legitimized by studying nurses in the context of a changing institutional environment. One of the first to show how language can be used in identity work, their study highlighted how the legitimation of a new professional role identity relied on arguments that maintained continuity with the past. This finding stood in stark contrast to previous research showing the importance of discrediting an old identity before change could occur.

Also studying identity work, Kyratsis et al. (2017) showed how professionals (physicians) responded to identity threats due to shifts in the professional logic leading to significant changes in their identity. While most studies consider professional identity in isolation from other aspects of social identity, Kyratsis et al.'s (2017) focus on Eastern European physicians in transitioning health systems showed that broader social identities can be critical to the process of constructing a new professional role identity. They showed that social identities broadly consistent with a new professional identity can provide an important resource that enables physicians to reconstruct their professional identity.

Reay et al. (2017) somewhat similarly showed how reinterpreting multiple logics and their relationships through different kinds of social interaction can result in changes in the professional role identity of physicians. However, in contrast to previous work suggesting that identity changes must be driven by professionals themselves, Reay et al. (2017) highlighted the agentic role of managers and other health professionals in arranging interactions to facilitate physician identity change. While previous papers assume a tight connection between roles and identity, Chreim et al. (2020) revealed how the dynamics of identity construction can support divergence from the professional roles in which people are trained. They show how counter-institutional identities can be developed and sustained through oppositional identity work combined with relational identity work, reinforcing superiority to "those who we are not."

Other studies using a healthcare context to consider how identity can be reconstructed have focused on professional role changes as a trigger for identity work. Croft, Currie, and Lockett (2015) studied identity conflict experienced by nurses as they transitioned into hybrid professional-managerial roles. In examining the nature of identity work associated with managing identity conflict, this study revealed important emotional challenges that altered nurses' responses to their new roles. In contrast to previous research suggesting that desired group identities facilitate the development of leader identities, Croft et al. (2015) showed that desired group identities can also undermine the construction of leader identities.

Also studying nurses' role transitions, Finn, Currie, and Martin (2010) examined changes in the delivery of genetic services in the English NHS, highlighting the tensions between individual and collective identity constructions. They found that the institutionalized hierarchy of healthcare provider roles constrained the ability of those in new occupational roles to construct a new identity. This study contributes to theory by showing that the interplay between individual and collective levels of identity is different in a professionalized context compared with other settings, and that this difference is an important factor in understanding identity dynamics.

A second set of papers advancing our understanding of identity focused on the ways that identity can be interwoven with a variety of organizational outcomes. While much of the identity literature suggests that identity frames are predicated on relationships between identity and action, these articles linking identity to outcomes specified the nature of this relationship. Several studies in our dataset focused on how occupational identities and other social identities interact in organizational settings. Kellogg (2012) showed how social identity-based status tactics were used by resistors to block an organizational reform initiative. While identity-based status had been previously shown to shape behavior, this study adds to our understanding of microlevel institutional change by showing how identity-based status can be used as a weapon to preserve the status quo.

Studying nurse and primary care technician dyads, DiBenigno and Kellogg (2014) found that collaboration between cross-occupational dyads was facilitated by other shared social identities such as shared race, age, or immigration status, which loosened attachment to occupational identities and status hierarchies. As part of their contributions, they suggested that previous studies of cross-occupational collaboration may have overstated the influence of occupational identity and status and understated the influence of other social identities.

Also focusing on conflict between groups with different occupational identities, DiBenigno (2018) showed how organizational structures can support groups to overcome identity differences and achieve shared subordinate goals. Investigating US Army commanders and mental health professionals, DiBenigno (2018) contributed to our understanding of identity conflict in organizations by highlighting how structure, rather than dynamics associated with identity, can help to resolve conflict between different occupational groups.

Finally, de Rond and Lok (2016) showed how a strong professional identity can lead to dysfunctional outcomes when the organizational conditions are not congruent with that identity. They studied physicians treating injured wartime soldiers in Afghanistan and found that organizational requirements producing dissonance with professional values contributed to physicians' experiences of psychological injury. They showed how expectations arising through the clash of professional socialization and actual lived organizational experiences can produce psychological distress.

Summary.   Research situated in healthcare contributes to theory about social identity in two ways. First, studies showed how new processes of identity work and identity can change, particularly with respect to professionals. Second, these articles provide important examples of how identity can influence the success or failure of desired organizational initiatives.

2.4 Networks

In contrast to much research in social science that focuses on the attributes of individual actors, social network theory promotes an alternative view: the attributes of individuals or organizations are less important for understanding their behavior than the pattern of relationships and ties they have with actors within their networks (Borgatti & Ofem, 2010). The results from many studies support this view, showing that networks facilitate the flow of information and influence, maintain social and professional norms, and have a substantial impact on the adoption of practices (Rogers, 2003).

The healthcare field has long been an important empirical setting for network studies (Valente & Pitts, 2017). This is because networks are especially important in complex arenas such as healthcare, where multiple organizations and professional groups, often with different beliefs, interests, and specialist roles, need to work together to develop and implement new ideas (D'Andreta et al., 2016). Indeed, Coleman, Katz, and Menzel's (1957) study of the role of network ties in promoting the adoption of a new medication among physicians was one of the earliest and most influential studies of social networks. Recent research has focused on the key role of brokers in social networks (Halevy, Halali, & Zlatev, 2019). These are individuals or organizations that occupy a bridging position between other actors who are not otherwise connected to each other in a network, thus providing the broker with opportunities to exert considerable influence on the behavior of these actors (Burt, Kilduff, & Tasselli, 2013). In other words, brokers straddle what Burt (1992) termed a structural hole.

The four studies in our dataset that we review here focus heavily on the role of brokers in healthcare organizations, advancing our understanding of the conditions under which brokers and network structure matter for two particular outcomes: (1) the transfer of knowledge for clinical care and (2) organizational change to improve clinical care. Currie and White (2012) showed that the effectiveness of brokers in promoting the use of evidence-based clinical practices depended in part on their professional status and position in the hierarchy of hospitals. Physicians who held higher-level posts as clinician-managers in NHS hospitals were better able to promote the use of evidence-based practices (for managing medication and transitions for elders) compared to nurses or other physicians who held managerial roles, but of lesser rank. Tasselli (2015) also examined brokers, their profession, and their roles in the transfer of knowledge in a hospital setting. He found that managers who held central broker positions in networks were able to effectively facilitate knowledge transfer between cliques of doctors and nurses, who typically did not communicate with each other. Further, similar to the findings of Currie and White (2012), the research showed that actors who were members of more than one clique (i.e., nurses and physicians who also had management roles) were more likely to occupy brokerage positions that enabled them to gain access to unique, valuable knowledge for patient care.

Battilana and Casciaro (2012) examined variation in the network position of individuals who aimed to initiate organizational changes in NHS hospitals. Their results showed that individuals with more opportunities to act as brokers (i.e., there were more structural holes in their networks) were better able to launch and promote the adoption of innovative changes. However, individuals with more holes in their networks also had less success in promoting the adoption of relatively routine changes in practices. Also investigating change initiatives, D'Andreta et al. (2016) showed that the ability of network structure to promote innovation in organizational practices depended on the cognitive frames or understandings that individuals held about proposed changes. In a comparative study of two networks of health-care providers, analyses showed that the network with more decentralized decision-making and members who interpreted the project's goals as support-ive of patient care was more effective than the network characterized by greater centralization and member interpretations of the project as a "research effort."

Summary.   Studies based on healthcare settings have contributed to network theory in two ways. First, researchers showed the importance of network structure and how brokers can effectively transfer knowledge across structural holes. Second, studies revealed ways in which the network position of brokers can facilitate processes of organizational change.

2.5 Diffusion of Innovation

In 1962 Everett Rogers published a book titled *Diffusion of Innovations*. It was a groundbreaking account that drew on social science to explain how and why innovations sometimes catch on and spread like wildfire, while others spread slowly, or not at all. In the original version, and in a series of updated editions, Rogers argued that innovations may be of different types – such as techno-logical, social, or ideas. Of particular interest for us in writing this Element, he drew on many examples from healthcare to illustrate his key points, such as the nondiffusion of knowledge that boiling water can eliminate many life-threatening diseases. He also showed how key stakeholders (British Navy captains) could distort the transfer of knowledge about vitamin C as a cure for scurvy. In addition, his work explained how different groups in organizations (such as hospitals) can be more or less likely to adopt new technologies (see Rogers, 2003).

All of these ideas have been further developed and integrated into different aspects of organization theory over time. Similar to the cases Rogers drew on, many empirical studies contributing to theory about the diffusion of innovation or knowledge transfer more generally have been situated in healthcare where there are countless examples of technological innovations, new medical knowledge, or new ways of providing care that have the potential to save lives, ameliorate pain, or improve efficiency. Since advanced technology plays such a critical role in providing a variety of services, researchers have been able to follow the trajectory of invention, prototype creation, testing, and implementation of new technologies (e.g., surgical machinery, pharmaceuticals), and more broadly to consider the spread of new ideas (such as advanced treatment knowledge) and the implementation of new ideas in practice.

Of particular note is the investigation by Ferlie et al. (2005), titled "The Nonspread of Innovations." This article drew on data concerning the diffusion (or not) of four different innovations in healthcare. The results showed a nonlinear pattern for the spread of innovation, with particular attention to the role of professionals in facilitating or blocking that spread. This work was formative in paving the way for future studies investigating the characteristics and trajectories of other innovations in healthcare and other settings. In addition, two important articles regarding the selective spread of Total Quality Management initiatives in hospitals (Kennedy & Fiss, 2009; Westphal, Gulati, & Shortell, 1997) showed how and why innovations (or parts thereof) can be picked up and implemented, or not. Adding to the knowledge base, researchers taking a social science approach focused on different aspects of diffusion, moving away from attention to technological innovations, by returning to some of the concepts identified by Rogers (2003) – attention to how ideas or knowledge can travel (Czarniawska & Joerges, 1995) and how knowledge can be transferred to practice (Ansari, Fiss, & Zajac, 2010). In this subsection we discuss articles based on healthcare studies that advanced organization theory in the following three categories: diffusion of technical innovations, knowledge transfer, and transfer of knowledge to practice.

Diffusion of technical innovations.   Consistent with the abundance of advances in healthcare stemming from the development of new technology, articles in our dataset develop theory about the diffusion of technical innovation in different ways. Compagni, Mele, and Ravasi (2014) showed how the process of introducing and implementing robotic surgery followed a path characterized by intermittent rounds of failure and success. They advanced theory by explaining how early experiences with innovations can influence later adoptions. Other articles focused on the role of proprietary rights to new technology, showing that patents can help to create evidence that leads to more effective treatment options (Vakili & McGahan, 2016), and that private firms' scientific publications about new pharmaceuticals can be a tool to market innovations and also improve profitability (Polidoro & Theeke, 2012).

In a final example of technology diffusion, Gardner, Boyer, and Ward (2017) studied the simultaneous use of technology and routines, revealing how the mindful use of technologies must occur in conjunction with supportive organizational routines to achieve desired outcomes. Collectively, these articles help to show that the way in which new technologies diffuse is significantly influenced by the organizational and institutional context.

Knowledge transfer.   Other articles in our dataset focus on the process of transferring knowledge from one location to another in ways that are consistent with the concept of the travel of ideas (Czarniawska & Joerges, 1995). A fundamental component of this approach is that ideas or concepts change as they travel, at least partly because ideas travel with people and as part of communication patterns. As a result, knowledge developed in one location or situation may be altered as it travels, and it may or may not be valuable in a new situation. For example, Tasselli (2015) studied patterns of knowledge transfer between physicians and nurses, showing how the same knowledge can be perceived and used differently depending on professional orientation.

Portraying knowledge transfer as a social dilemma, Wilkesmann, Wilkesmann, and Virgillito (2009) surveyed hospital employees to investigate cultural and motivational factors associated with knowledge transfer. They showed that direct channels for interaction, supportive organizational culture, and intrinsic motivation of employees are required for the effective transfer of knowledge. In a different approach to examining the knowledge transfer process, Van Grinsven, Sturdy, and Heusinkveld (2020) focused on the role of identity work as a mechanism for translating management concepts as part of implementing "lean" in hospital contexts. They found that managers developed identity narratives that facilitated an effective translation and knowledge transfer process.

Finally, in their investigation of the geographic travel of healthcare knowledge from India to the Cayman Islands, Gupta and Khanna (2019) developed a theoretical model showing the importance of a recombination–replication–adaptation tradeoff that could be applied to other situations of international knowledge transfer. Collectively, these articles advance theory about knowledge transfer by showing the critical role of key actors who appropriately modify concepts within their context as part of an effective translation process.

Transfer of knowledge to practice.   Several papers used healthcare settings to advance arguments about how new ideas can be translated into practice. Reay et al. (2013) examined the processes by which the concept of "interdisciplinary teamwork" became institutionalized as new practice in primary care clinics. Their longitudinal case studies show that transitioning from knowledge to practice required three managerial-led activities: microlevel theorizing, encouraging trying new practices, and facilitating collective meaning-making. A key element of this model is that longer-term success relied on moving from a "good idea" to a habitualized practice through the trial and repetition of desired activities over time.

Somewhat similarly, Nigam, Huising, and Golden (2016) examined organizational (hospital) initiatives to change work routines in response to new knowledge about better ways to provide services. They found that ongoing engagement by elite actors (those with authority and influence) was essential to success. Paying more attention to the role of elite actors, Greenwood et al. (2019) showed how physicians with expertise markers could act as influential agents in promoting the adoption of new best practices. Finally, Raman and Bharadwaj (2012) investigated practice transfer processes to reveal how power differentials can derail well-designed initiatives. Overall, these studies show the importance of key agents within organizations who hold the power and influence to encourage or derail processes designed to move knowledge to practice.

Summary.   Studies in healthcare contexts have been critical in developing organization theory about the spread and uptake of new technology, knowledge transfer, and the ways in which frontline practices embed (or not) these new advances. Research on the diffusion of new technologies highlighted the important role of the organizational and institutional context, while studies investigating knowledge transfer have focused on the key actors who modify concepts in order to develop an effective translation process. Research examining how new knowledge can be embedded in frontline practices has shown the important role of powerful agents and how they can impact the outcome of processes designed to transfer knowledge into practice.

2.6 Organizational Change

A final set of articles we discuss in this section address different aspects of organizational change. We take a broad view of organizational change, describing it as a process in which an organization, or a subset of an organization, changes its operational approach, technologies, structure, or strategies. There is a long tradition in organization theory of seeking to understand and predict various aspects of organizational change; the studies in our dataset build on the multiple perspectives from which change has been addressed.

In our dataset, we identified articles examining processes of organizational change from the following perspectives: (1) how different ways of collaborating, coordinating, or interacting can lead to organizational change, (2) how restructuring or redesigning work is associated with organizational change, (3) how organizational processes or outcomes can be improved through change initiatives, and (4) how processes of sensemaking can impact organizational change. We will now discuss each of these topics.

A number of articles focused on understanding processes of collaboration, coordination, and interaction, investigating how different ways of working together can be associated with organizational change, or the lack of change. Pine and Mazmanian (2016) investigated the implementation of an electronic health records system in a hospital obstetric unit. They showed how the requirements of using the electronic health records negatively impacted the previously established ways of coordinating care, and resulted in "contorted coordination" that left healthcare providers struggling to deliver quality services. Also investigating the impact of technology, Aristidou and Barrett (2018) examined changes at the practice level in the UK mental health system. They showed how technology platforms (such as computer-, phone-, network-, or internet-based) impacted how patterns of interaction among healthcare providers were constantly reconfigured over time. They highlighted the importance of the following processes: spanning time, stretching space, and distributed agency – all contributing to the development of a process model explaining how practice change can occur.

Focusing on boundary-spanning activities, Kislov, Hyde, and McDonald (2017) studied collaborative arrangements between a university and connected healthcare organizations, with a focus on boundary-spanning roles. They showed how changes in the structure, sources, and mutual convertibility of capital assets over time could alter healthcare roles and practices, leading to overall change for the organization and the health system. Somewhat similarly, Caldwell, Roehrich, and George (2017) examined public–private collaborations in the UK health sector, building theory about organizational change by revealing how the engagement of professionals (especially physicians) is critical to improvements in task performance. An important caveat they found was that professional engagement must be tailored to the particulars of the public–private partnership model for desired organizational changes to be effectively implemented.

Finally, the following two articles also investigated how interactions are related to change initiatives. Dupret (2018) focused on the importance of performative silences as part of organizational change processes. Through an ethnographic study in a mental healthcare organization, the study revealed how different performances of silence can facilitate new decision-making processes in the organization and influence the development of new work practices – all impacting ways that change unfolds. Also interested in interactions within organizations, McGivern et al. (2017) investigated a management consultancy project involving diverse professional and occupational groups in a UK healthcare organization. They found that each participating group (consultants, managers, professional groups) conceptualized time for accomplishing the desired changes in different ways, leading to negative consequences for the organizational change process overall.

In the second set of articles considering organizational change, three studies focused on restructuring or redesign initiatives. Dattée and Barlow (2017) used data from "whole-system" healthcare change in Scotland to develop theory about the multilevel dynamics underlying organizational adaptation. They drew on complexity theory to show how local change agents were guided by top-down rules that set out expectations for frontline actions, while at the same time creating conditions enabling professionals and others within the healthcare system to engage in bottom-up changes at the practice level. More focused on restructuring, Wiedner and Mantere (2019) investigated changes in the UK healthcare system to develop a process model of how organizations can divest or spin off units in order to establish autonomous entities that more effectively provide services. As a result, they developed theory about organizational separation processes and organizational autonomy in relation to organizational change. Paying attention to work redesign, Van Offenbeek, Sorge, and Knip (2009) showed how the introduction of a new position (nurse practitioner) impacted professional and political dynamics in ways that led to varying degrees of organizational change in different subunits of a Dutch hospital.

A third set of articles addressing aspects of organizational change focused on improving organizational processes or outcomes. These fall into two categories: organizational learning and performance improvement. Regarding organizational learning, Nembhard and Tucker (2011) investigated dynamic service settings (hospitals) to show how the implementation of deliberate learning activities could improve organizational outcomes. Desai (2014) also focused on organizational learning by studying failures and successes in California hospitals where heart bypass surgery was performed. He drew on the principles of attribution theory to explain how organizational experiences influence an organization's ability to learn. In later work, Desai (2020) studied organizational learning in hospital emergency departments in California. The findings showed that busy organizations with increasingly constrained capacity (i.e., spikes of overload in emergency departments) are less able to learn than organizations with consistently constrained capacity (consistently busy emergency departments). Clark, Huckman, and Staats (2013) studied volume-based learning in the context of radiologists who provided reports (readings) to hospitals on an outsourced basis. They showed that radiologists learned to improve performance through their cross-organizational connections with the hospitals that paid them for their work, benefiting both the radiologists and the hospitals.

Focusing on organizational performance, King et al. (2011) analyzed data from employee and patient surveys, census data, and performance indexes for 142 UK hospitals. They showed that levels of ethnic diversity in the community relative to the ethnic diversity of the hospital workforce influenced organizational performance; the degree to which diversity within the organization was representative of the community was positively related to civility experienced by patients and ultimately enhanced organizational performance. Maltarich et al. (2017) examined the impact of pay-for-performance on healthcare employees, showing how individual responses to financial incentives can contribute to changes in overall organizational performance. Finally, Gardner et al. (2017) analyzed time-sequenced data from 262 US hospitals investigating performance improvement in clinical care quality. They showed how the mindful use of information technologies and adherence to specified routines were positively associated with organizational performance.

In a final subcategory, four articles drew on the concept of sensemaking to advance theory about organizational change. Lockett et al. (2013) focused their attention on the actions of three focal actors who were located in different social positions in the English NHS. All were tasked with enacting a common organizational change. The findings revealed how the actors engaged differently in sensemaking as a result of their social position, and how these differences impacted their ability to manage organizational change. Heaphy (2017) studied patient advocates in hospitals and developed a process model showing how individual actors can engage in sensemaking and sensegiving, thus facilitating organizational change through the development of more collaborative relationships with clients. Focusing on team performance, Antino, Rico, and Thatcher (2019) gathered data from 271 employees and 41 leaders in 41 healthcare teams to assess outcomes. Their findings revealed how team fault lines (as informal sensemaking structures) could threaten perceptions of team justice and negatively influence overall performance. Somewhat similarly, Christianson (2019) investigated sensemaking through intensive analysis of interactions in emergency department teams that engaged in rapid decision-making processes when faced with a critical patient concern. The findings showed how different processes of collective sensemaking can lead to significant differences in team performance that impact a healthcare organization's ability to provide quality care.

Summary.   Articles investigating different aspects of organizational change in healthcare settings focused on micro- and mesolevel analyses to explain how different ways of collaborating, coordinating, or interacting can lead to organizational change. Other studies engaged in analyses at the organizational level, showing how restructuring or redesigning work can impact organizational change initiatives. In addition, some research focused attention on how organizational processes or outcomes can be improved through change initiatives. Finally, a subset of articles investigated how processes of sensemaking can impact change in organizations.

2.7 Section Summary

To conclude this section, we return to our initial reasons for analyzing the prevalence and content of articles based on healthcare settings that have been published in select organization journals. We wanted to know if the number of articles was increasing over time, and we wanted to understand the ways in which these articles contributed to theory. We note that we found a substantial number of publications, with a total of seventy-five articles identified; however, it is not clear if the trend is clearly upward (see Figure 1). The breadth of topics addressed is interesting. We expected to find a relatively large number of articles contributing to institutional theory, and we did. However, we also found almost as many articles that contributed to the literature on professions and the diffusion of innovation. In addition, there were a large number of articles focused on a broad range of topics related to organizational change. Overall, it is clear that many aspects of healthcare settings provide rich opportunities for the development of organization theory. The highly institutionalized context, the presence of powerful actors at all levels of analysis, a highly professionalized workforce, and the seemingly never-ending change initiatives in healthcare all contribute to the potential for excellent research studies, and are likely to do so for the foreseeable future.

3 How Healthcare Studies Use Organization Theory

An important aim of this Element is to encourage healthcare researchers to increase their use of organization theory to advance knowledge about the provision of healthcare services. In Section 1 we highlighted Lewin's (1951) emphasis on the practical value of theory, and here we specifically argue that theory-informed healthcare research can produce important insights for managers, policy-makers, and clinicians that they otherwise would have overlooked. In order to assess the use of organization theory in related healthcare research articles, we gathered the citation records of articles in our dataset that were published between 2009 and 2015, allowing time for the integration of ideas into healthcare research. For each article, we recorded the total citations and citation counts in the following selected journals because they have a well-established tradition of attention to theory: *Health Care Management Review*;

Medical Care Research and Review; *Health Services Research*; *Milbank Quarterly*; and *Social Science and Medicine* (see Table 1 for total citation counts and citations in these healthcare journals).

The number of citations in these healthcare journals is very low. Although the organization theory articles in our dataset are well cited overall (citations range from 12 to 1,630), the number of citations in the healthcare journals ranges from zero to seventeen, with an average of 2.27 citations per article. Approximately 25 percent of these citations fall into the category of self-citations by the small set of authors who typically publish in both organizational and healthcare journals.

In response to this disconnect between theory development articles in organization journals and articles published in healthcare journals, we next looked more broadly at publications in healthcare journals. To accomplish this wider examination of healthcare journals, we extended our literature search to include articles we believed provided important exemplars; as a result, our presentation in this section includes articles from 2003 to 2020. We focus our discussion here on articles that exemplify how healthcare management researchers have used organization theory to motivate research questions and problems and, importantly, to develop practical knowledge related to improvement in the access to, cost, and quality of healthcare services. To identify articles for this review, we looked across the six healthcare journals noted at the start of this section, and identified four theoretical approaches that appeared most often in these journals (institutional theory; resource dependence theory; transaction cost theory; and theories of organizational change). We then chose examples of each approach to illustrate how researchers studying healthcare contexts can use theory to advance their work.

We note that the articles we review in subsections 3.1 to 3.4 draw on organizational theories that differ somewhat from those we discussed earlier. For example, although our literature search for Section 2 did not show any articles using resource dependence theory, healthcare management researchers have used this theory relatively commonly in their work. As we discuss in Section 4, the differential use of organizational theories in theory development vs. healthcare-focused journals may reveal important opportunities for future research.

3.1 Institutional Theory

The first category of healthcare articles we discuss are those employing concepts from institutional theory. We focus on six articles that use institutional theory to understand important initiatives to improve healthcare systems in five nations – the US, the UK, Canada, the Netherlands, and Sweden.

Two articles use institutional theory to analyze US hospitals, one focusing on their adoption of electronic health records (Fareed et al., 2015), and another examining the formation of Accountable Care Organizations (Goodrick & Reay, 2016). Focusing on national initiatives, Macfarlane et al. (2013) use institutional theory to analyze changes in the UK NHS. Berghout et al. (2018) also focused on a national level of analysis, using concepts of institutional work to examine the role that physician leaders in the Netherlands played in a national program to improve healthcare there. Quartz-Topp, Sanne, and Pöstges (2018) drew on the concept of institutional logics in their case study of quality improvement projects in a Swedish and a Dutch hospital. Last, Gray et al. (2017) examined the responses of community-based home care providers to a Canadian government policy launched to increase their accountability.

We begin with Fareed et al. (2015) and Gray et al. (2017), who both used Oliver's (1991) conceptual model to examine the extent to which healthcare organizations comply with institutional pressures stemming from government policies. Drawing on both institutional theory and resource dependence theory, Oliver argued that organizational responses to external pressure can vary widely from "failure to comply" to "full compliance."

The results from regression analyses of data from over 2,000 US hospitals between 2005 and 2009 mainly showed support for the model (Fareed et al., 2015). In particular, the results show that hospital adoption of electronic health records was not due only to the technical advantages they conferred for patient care – rather, the need to maintain their legitimacy and gain access to resources that are associated with legitimacy (e.g., financial incentives to use electronic health records from the federal government) also motivated hospital behavior. Further, the results suggested that hospitals engaged in mimetic behavior – imitating the adoption patterns of neighboring hospitals.

Gray et al. (2017) examined the responsiveness of community care agencies operating in Ontario, Canada to a new government-imposed requirement for accountability. The results from analyses of survey data from 114 care agencies showed that organizational responses to the new policy ranged from active compliance to noncompliance. Although the majority of organizations changed internal policies, practices, or procedures to meet new government require-ments for increased accountability, 44 percent did not accept contracts with the government, thus avoiding any changes. The results also showed that environ-mental factors, such as the presence of an association representing organiza-tional interests, influenced bargaining tactics.

In a conceptual article, Goodrick and Reay (2016) argued that the formal mission of Accountable Care Organizations inherently forces them to face the critical challenge of managing multiple institutional logics. Accountable Care Organizations are the result of US policy to improve efficiency and effectiveness in healthcare. They are a group of healthcare providers that work together and receive a financial bonus from the Centers for Medicare and Medicaid Services if they meet targets for cost control and quality of patient care. Specifically, the "triple aim" mission of these organizations is to (a) improve patient experience of care (including quality and satisfaction), (b) improve the health of populations, and (c) reduce the per capita cost of healthcare. Goodrick and Reay argued that each element of this "triple aim" corresponds to a different institutional logic – the professional, state, and market logics, respectively. Accountable Care Organizations thus can be viewed as organizations charged with the goal of combining different logics available in society "under one organizational roof" (Jay, 2013).

Further, drawing on prior research in institutional theory (e.g., Greenwood et al., 2011; Kraatz & Block, 2008), Goodrick and Reay suggested three options for Accountable Care Organizations to effectively manage multiple logics. First, they could find ways to reinterpret practices traditionally associated with one logic to make them compatible with other logics (e.g., improving patient experience through patient-centered care can help to cut costs if patients take more control of their health). Second, they could engage in strategies that take advantage of existing synergy between conflicting logics (e.g., financial incentives can possibly motivate providers to improve care quality). Third, they could create opportunities for frontline healthcare providers to develop innovative ways of working that combine multiple logics. For example, multidisciplinary teamwork in primary care settings can mean that physicians take on a coordinating rather than "hands-on" role, allowing other (less expensive) professionals to provide services and increasing the total number of patients receiving care.

Macfarlane and his colleagues (2013) conducted an ambitious empirical study using institutional theory to analyze a large-scale effort that aimed to substantially change the norms, culture, and structure of the UK NHS. They conducted a secondary analysis of data using a mixed-method, longitudinal case study design. Specifically, they compared data (activity statistics, documents, interviews, surveys, site visits) gathered from the post-change period (2010–11) to data from the pre-change initiative period (2003–8). These researchers relied particularly on Scott's (2014) model of the three "institutional pillars" (regulative, normative, and cultural-cognitive) to analyze their data.

Berghout et al. (2018) drew on concepts related to institutional work to analyze the role that physician leaders played in efforts to reform the national healthcare system in the Netherlands (e.g., increase reliance on performance metrics). These researchers systematically examined the discourse of physician leaders (e.g., heads of national professional bodies) in key documents to understand how they responded to policy changes, and, in particular, how they aimed to influence the behavior of "rank-and-file" physicians. The results showed that physician leaders aimed to persuade their colleagues to retake control of the medical professions; drop "old" professional values (e.g., become "team players"); and build a new identity for the "modern" physician (e.g., one who leads in quality improvement and cost control).

Last, Quartz-Topp et al. (2018) conducted a case study to understand how hospital managers can create "hybrid practices" to support quality improvement programs. These are practices that combine both managerial and clinical per-spectives on how to improve the quality of care, thereby gaining support from clinicians. The results from a case study that involved both a Swedish and a Dutch hospital showed that managers were able to design forums, tools, and professional roles to facilitate the integration of both a managerial and clinical perspective on quality improvement. The authors argued that their observations support the view that managers can engage in institutional work specifically aimed at creating logics that bridge the worldviews of clinicians' and managers' hybrid logics (Greenwood et al., 2011).

The results from these six articles suggest three important conclusions. First, accounting for the complex pattern of change and inertia that the data show requires using all three of Scott's pillars and analyzing the interplay between macro-institutional structures (at the national level) and individual agency (at the local level). Second, the results show that institutional theory can be applied usefully at an organizational level to understand how healthcare organizations and their managers achieve change and what factors promote or hinder efforts to sustain changes. Third, although change did not occur easily, the data suggest that both normative and mimetic forces for change can be powerful, and that top managers' and leaders' strategic use of rhetoric, including the deliberate use of language and storytelling, effectively promoted change.

Summary.   These articles produce insights that are useful for managers, clinicians, and policy-makers. First, the results we reviewed suggest that policy-makers can strengthen their efforts to promote the use of information technol-ogy, for example by providing incentives for respected peer hospitals to be role models for nearby neighbors. Second, these articles suggest practical ways for managers and clinicians to mitigate conflicts that arise from competing logics in their professions, for example by strategically creating multidisciplinary teams to reorganize clinical work to satisfy competing demands to improve care quality and cost. Third, the results we reviewed suggest that fundamental change in healthcare systems is more likely to occur, and to be sustained, when key actors at the clinical, organizational, and government levels use multiple levers to promote change. In turn, this means that traditional efforts to promote change that rely heavily on top-down regulations will not be as effective as interventions that also aim to change norms and cultural and cognitive models "on the ground."

3.2 Resource Dependence Theory

Resource dependence theory views organizations as open systems that engage in exchanges with actors in their external environment for needed resources (Davis & Cobb, 2010; Pfeffer & Salancik, 1978). In the course of these exchanges, a focal organization becomes more or less dependent on its exchange partners (Emerson, 1962). Specifically, dependence in exchange relationships is a function of two key factors: the extent to which an exchange partner controls a valued resource, and whether the resource is relatively scarce – it has few other providers. When these factors characterize an exchange, one partner holds a power advantage in the relationship, thus threatening key resources for the dependent partner. Faced with such conditions, organizations aim to maximize their autonomy by engaging in a range of strategic responses that reduce their dependence on external actors, including mergers and acquisitions; diversifying; lobbying to alter rules and regulations that govern exchange relationships; and hiring critical personnel.

Further, in their widely influential book, *The External Control of Organizations: A Resource Dependence Perspective*, Pfeffer and Salancik (1978) argued that organizations aim to reduce uncertainty in exchange relationships, especially when critical resources are at stake. Uncertainty stems from environments that are unstable, that lack resources in general, or that involve complex relationships among a range of actors (Dess & Beard, 1984). Healthcare organizations often face environments with these characteristics, which may account for the popularity of resource dependence theory among healthcare researchers.

In this subsection, we review four papers published in healthcare journals that use resource dependence theory to examine healthcare providers' responses to their environments. Two papers focus on the relationship between key environmental conditions and the adoption of information technology (electronic health records) by hospitals and physician groups, and two papers consider how hospital environments relate to their performance on the dimensions of cost, quality, and access to care.

Menachemi and colleagues (2011, 2012) conducted two studies that examined relationships between organizations' environments and their adoption of health information technology. The results from a 2011 national study of US hospitals showed that the type of vendors they selected for their information systems varied depending on the environments they faced. Hospitals working in poor-resource environments chose single vendors – an efficient strategy. In contrast, hospitals facing more complex and uncertain environments were more likely to select specialized vendors – a strategy that aimed to match vendor strengths to particular hospital needs. In a similar study, Menachemi and colleagues (2012) examined the adoption of information technology by a US national sample of physician groups. The results showed that physician groups facing more threatening, dynamic, and complex environments (high levels of unemployment, poverty, and malpractice rates) were less likely to adopt the technology compared to physician groups located in more stable environments.

Two studies use resource dependence theory to examine the operating environments of US hospitals and their performance on measures of efficiency, quality of care, and provision of services for individuals without means to pay for them. Yeager, Zhang, and Diana (2015) show that hospitals operating in more resource-rich and competitive environments are more likely to participate in Accountable Care Organizations and thus focus on meeting targets for cost control and quality of patient care.

Hsieh, Clement, and Bazzoli (2010) examined the relationship between key aspects of hospitals' environments and two important measures of performance: efficiency and provision of services for patients without means to pay (uncompensated care). The results showed that hospitals were responsive to demands from their local environments: they provided more uncompensated care when demand increased for these services. At the same time, hospitals that were more dependent on payment from government insurers (Medicare or Medicaid) were both less efficient and provided less uncompensated care – likely because Medicare and Medicaid patients have more complex, chronic, and expensive health conditions.

In concluding this subsection, we note that Yeager et al. (2014) reviewed the healthcare management literature with the aim of understanding how researchers have used resource dependence theory to empirically examine the external environments of healthcare organizations. This review of twenty papers showed relatively strong support for hypotheses derived from resource dependence theory that examined the relationship between conditions in organizational environments and the outcomes of interest, reinforcing the practical value of this theory for healthcare research.

Summary.   Taken together, the results from these studies provide an important message for policy-makers: the extent to which healthcare providers participate in programs that aim to improve their performance depends, at least in part, on the circumstances they face in local environments. As a result, policy initiatives that rely heavily on "one-size-fits-all" incentives to change the behavior of healthcare providers are likely to fall short of their goals. Resource dependence makes a difference. The results from these studies also hold implications for managers: more so than in the past, effective organizational performance may hinge on their ability to monitor and respond to changing patterns of resource dependence that stem from relationships with a range of external actors, including payers, information technology vendors, competitors, and local communities.

3.3 Transaction Cost Theory

Building on the seminal work of two Nobel laureates (Coase, 1937; Williamson, 1975, 1985), transaction cost theory has become one of the most influential theories in organization and management studies (Cuypers, Hennart, Silverman, & Ertug, 2020). It was first developed to analyze organizational decisions to engage in vertical integration, specifically by "making" – producing a service or product internally – vs. "buying" – contracting with external organizations for needed resources. Researches have since employed transaction cost theory to analyze a broad range of organizational phenomena, including diversification, multinational firms, strategic alliances, supply-chain relationships, and public–private partnerships.

Transaction cost theory is similar to resource dependence theory in its focus on exchanges that organizations engage in with key actors in their environments to obtain needed resources. Rather than a resource dependence focus on power dynamics in these exchanges, transaction cost analysis focuses on the costs involved in creating and maintaining these ties. Specifically, transaction costs are defined as costs involved in negotiating, monitoring, and enforcing the terms of an exchange, through contracts or more informal means. A fundamental premise is that organizations and managers aim to minimize these costs.

Further, the theory argues that three key attributes of exchanges drive transaction costs: asset specificity (the extent to which resources are specialized), uncertainty, and frequency. When transaction costs are high because of these attributes of exchanges, organizations will respond by seeking to manage costs through ownership and bureaucratic systems of control – this is the "make" strategy in vertical integration (Williamson, 1985). In contrast, when transaction costs are low, organizations can rely on market transactions (buying through contracts) to protect their interests.

We review three papers in this subsection that use transaction cost theory to examine a fundamental question in the healthcare field: how to effectively and efficiently organize the diverse services that patients need to promote the quality of care they receive. Although each paper examines a distinctive empirical context (nursing homes; hospitals and patient safety; Accountable Care Organizations), they share a focus on vertical integration; that is, the linking of healthcare providers who provide distinctive services for patients.

First, Zinn and her colleagues (2003) use transaction cost theory to analyze the conditions under which healthcare providers use vertical integration as a strategy to coordinate services (i.e., the "make or buy" decision) between nursing homes and therapists providing rehabilitation services when federal payment for these services tightened. The results from regression analyses of national, longitudinal data on nursing homes showed support for hypotheses derived from transaction cost theory. Transaction frequency, uncertainty, and complexity prompted nursing homes to increase their control over therapy services by employing these professionals as opposed to outside contracting. In short, nursing homes acted to limit transaction costs by either exiting the market for rehabilitation services or exerting greater control over these services by managing them in-house.

Mick and Shay (2016) used a transaction cost approach to develop propositions about the conditions under which healthcare organizations will use Accountable Care Organizations to vertically integrate services (e.g., directly provide inpatient rehabilitation services) or engage in market exchanges with other providers. Their analysis has three main points. First, they argued that the decision to make (internalize) or buy (market exchanges) oversimplifies the likely range of possible arrangements that can comprise an Accountable Care Organization. For example, these organizations can use informal agreements to integrate services, such as agreeing to share electronic health records. Second, Mick and Shay outlined key factors that contribute to transaction costs in these settings, including uncertainty and complexity; similarly, they note that effective governance of relationships among the organizations (e.g., a governing board) will require resources. Last, this paper develops arguments and propositions about whether, when, and how entities will integrate as Accountable Care Organizations, and how they should do so to minimize transaction costs.

Fareed and Mick (2011), drawing on both resource dependence and transaction cost theories, focused on how hospitals respond to demands for improved patient safety by developing the capacity for patient safety programs internally (make) or contracting with outside specialists (buy). They develop propositions about factors that affect hospital decisions to adopt patient safety innovations (e.g., hospitals will be more likely to adopt innovative patient safety programs when faced with competitive and resource-rich environments and dependence on government insurance programs). Next, Fareed and Mick argued that most hospitals internalize their innovations in patient safety programs rather than approach the market, a choice that helps hospitals economize on transaction costs. Since this paper's publication, much evidence has accumulated to support this view.

Summary. The papers reviewed here show how researchers can usefully employ transaction cost theory to examine the antecedents of vertical integration for a wide array of healthcare organizations, including hospitals, nursing homes, and physician groups. Further, these papers argued that transaction costs in the healthcare field are typically substantial enough for organizations to respond by internalizing (making) services, rather than contracting for them. Consistent with this view, we indeed observe a continuing rise in mergers and acquisitions in the US healthcare field; similarly, in the US there has been a significant increase in the number of physicians who are employed by large hospital-led systems. Yet, in an excellent review of research on vertical integration in healthcare, Post, Buchmueller, and Ryan (2017) concluded that there is little empirical evidence to support its effectiveness for the quality or cost of care. Why do we observe this disconnect? Addressing this question should be a priority for research.

3.4 Theories of Organizational Change

In this final set of articles for Section 3, we discuss how healthcare researchers have addressed different aspects of organizational change. As noted in Section 2, we take a broad view of organizational change, describing it as a process in which an organization, or a subset of an organization, changes its operational approach, technologies, structure, or strategies.

We identified three articles examining processes of organizational change from the following perspectives: (1) how mindfulness among individual nurses and nursing teams can lower workarounds that increase nurses' work-related injuries; (2) how to involve clinical and support staff members to generate innovative ideas for hospital-improving performance; (3) how leadership in healthcare teams can promote relational coordination that, in turn, improves patient outcomes. Next, we discuss each of these topics.

Dierynck et al. (2016) examined the role of nurses' mindfulness in reducing their use of workarounds that did not conform to safety regulations and that, in turn, were a cause of work-related injuries. Prior work defines mindfulness as the ability to be fully conscious of what we are doing and where we are, and to be open to our current experience in a setting (Vogus & Sutcliffe, 2012). The results from multilevel modeling of survey data from 580 nurses across 54 nursing work teams showed that both individual and collective mindfulness were associated with lower rates of safety failures by reducing nurses' use of workarounds.

Building on prior work showing that frontline staff are both aware of deficiencies in operations and motivated to improve them (Tucker et al., 2008) and that using suggestions from frontline staff members can improve the quality of care (Nembhard & Tucker, 2011), Jung, Blasco, and Lakhani (2020) organized an innovation contest for clinical and support staff in a hospital cardiac center. The results from the contest showed that staff members submitted and evaluated a wide range of ideas for improving patient experience, cost of care, workflow, and access to services. Most importantly, staff participation in the contest and the overall success of the initiative depended on two key factors: the extent to which individuals believed that it was safe to speak up, and the extent to which they believed that new ideas were not tested frequently enough.

Huber, Rodriguez, and Shortell (2020) examined the role of leaders in facilitating teamwork, change, and relational coordination in sixteen primary care practices associated with two Accountable Care Organizations. The results from multilevel regression analyses of survey data from clinicians and staff members showed that effective leadership directly promoted relational coordination among members of primary care team members, independent of several other factors (e.g., team size). These results underscore the importance of team leaders who are skillful in facilitating change, especially because prior work showed that relational coordination is linked to several important measures of team effectiveness in healthcare organizations (Gittell, 2002a, 2002b).

Summary.   These papers show that efforts to improve the performance of healthcare organizations by changing their internal operations depend on several key factors. These include: effective leadership for change; the ability of organization members to be mindful in their work; and the extent to which individuals feel a psychological sense of safety in speaking up to challenge established practices and contribute new ideas (Edmondson, 1999). Further, these studies draw effectively on relatively well-established lines of research, including both concepts and methods, much of which has been conducted in healthcare settings. We note that, in contrast to other research reviewed in this section, these studies focus on levers for change and performance improvement that are internal to organizations, thus making them useful for managers aiming to improve coordination, innovation, and safety.

3.5 Section Summary

In this section we reviewed sixteen articles published in several leading health-care journals that used organization theory to motivate research questions and problems and, importantly, to develop practical knowledge to improve access to, and the cost and quality of, healthcare services. We observe that some common themes cut across these studies, despite their varying conceptual approaches and empirical contexts.

First, government policy has limits in its ability to change and improve healthcare systems, organizations, and services. The results from studies that examined policy initiatives in several nations that aimed to improve organizations' use of information technology, patient safety and quality programs, and coordination of care all show mixed results. In particular, the results suggest that policies may lack incentives that are strong enough to promote organizational change and, further, policies may not be tailored adequately enough to matter in local circumstances. Indeed, many studies showed that both local market and organizational characteristics substantially influence the extent to which policy initiatives reached their objectives. In particular, there is evidence that managers have responded strategically to market conditions by reducing transaction costs and dependence in their organizations' external relationships.

Second, these studies reveal strategic behavior on the part of local and national managers and leaders that effectively promoted change in systems and within organizations. These behaviors included the use of well-planned rhetoric and framing of issues to mobilize critical actors, creating practices and logics to support change efforts involving multiple stakeholders, involving frontline staff in problem-solving and innovation, and employing effective leadership skills to facilitate change.

In sum, our view is that these articles, taken together, provide compelling evidence to support more prevalent use of organization theory to inform research that examines a broad range of healthcare contexts and challenges for national systems as well as local organizations. In addition, we suggest that the incorporation of more recent theory development could improve healthcare research even further. We turn to a discussion of prospects for future research in the concluding Section 4.

4 Conclusions and Future Research Opportunities

In this Element, we have considered how research conducted in healthcare contexts has contributed to advancing organization theory, as well as how researchers have used organization theory to advance knowledge about the provision of healthcare services. While there are a relatively small number of organizational scholars who have investigated healthcare settings to advance their research, we see that more recent developments in organization theory are making healthcare settings increasingly desirable. We suggest that there is continually growing interest and acceptance of the idea that organizational scholars can learn about organizations and management from a variety of settings, not only the stereotypical business cases. For example, organizational journals now commonly publish articles based on research in a wide variety of settings such as war zones, refugee camps, government agencies, and presidential election processes. This shift has had the effect of making healthcare settings seem less unusual.

At the same time, there are other developments in organization theory that have made healthcare contexts, in particular, more desirable. For example, there has been increasing interest in professionals, institutional change, micro–macro connections, and technology, all of which can be productively studied in healthcare contexts. The inherent characteristics of healthcare settings, such as the ongoing existence of multiple stakeholders with different values, the large numbers of professionals employed in healthcare, the highly resilient systems that result in extreme resistance to change, the critical macro–micro connections required for delivery of services, and the ongoing imperative for new technology, make healthcare contexts particularly good locations for developing the theories that currently dominate organization and management studies.

Consequently, we see that research in healthcare settings can facilitate the advancement of theory by drawing on the specific characteristics of the context to explain the theoretical importance of findings. For example, researchers have argued that the exceptional level of stability in healthcare that is important to ensure reliable quality of care makes the setting an ideal location to study institutional change because it is so unlikely to occur. Similarly, the highly professionalized nature of healthcare provides researchers with a setting that is particularly well suited to studying dynamics between and among different professional groups. The findings from such research conducted in healthcare are relatively easily transferrable to other settings characterized by a professionalized workforce. In addition, the multi-level interconnections in healthcare (the tight linkages between patient care, the organizations where care is delivered, and the system level where principles and rules are established) make the setting an excellent research location to study micro–macro dynamics of change that are of particular interest to practice theory and related topics such as practice-driven institutionalism.

These same characteristics of healthcare settings mean that it is a less optimal location for some types of organizational research. The stability associated with healthcare can make it a difficult setting to study entrepreneurship or processes of organizational startup. The well-established ways of providing services mean that innovation in healthcare usually occurs very differently compared with other organizations such as Fortune 500 companies. Similarly, the importance of goals not related to profit that are critical in healthcare can make it difficult for scholars to generalize findings from healthcare settings to the broader business sector. Finally, we point out that the highly professionalized nature of healthcare workplaces can make it difficult to study organizational dynamics that are not impacted by external professional responsibilities and interprofessional relationships.

These particular aspects of healthcare also mean that organizational researchers must invest time and energy to understand the nuances of settings they are examining. Jumping into organizational research in a hospital setting, for example, can lead to insightful new discoveries when researchers understand the complexity of hospitals and the healthcare system in which they are embedded; but when they are oblivious to these nuances, disappointing or even inaccurate results may occur.

In addition, we point to the importance of considering differences in approaches to the provision of healthcare services across countries. Most of the articles we reviewed for this Element were based on research conducted in North America and Europe. Researchers should also pay close attention to similarities and differences that exist in other locations. Further, we note that most studies focus on healthcare services provided in hospitals or physician clinics. Other areas of healthcare, such as mental health and addictions, are in great need of research attention; however, investigating such areas also requires close attention to the significantly different context within which these services are provided.

By way of summarizing our findings in previous sections of this Element, we remind readers that in Section 2 we illustrated ways in which research in healthcare settings has successfully contributed to theory by examining articles published in the *Academy of Management Journal, Administrative Science Quarterly, Organization Science, Journal of Management Studies,* and *Organization Studies*. We identified six broad theoretical areas where there has been significant empirical research focused on healthcare settings: institutional theory; professions and organizations; social identity; networks; diffusion of innovation; and organizational change. In subsections 4.1 to 4.6 we present a summary of research in each of these areas that relies on healthcare contexts to contribute to organization theory, discuss areas for future research, and propose research questions that so far remain unexplored.

4.1 Institutional Theory

Summary.   Our survey of articles in organizational journals shows how research conducted in healthcare contexts has advanced institutional theory. Researchers have taken advantage of the embedded nature of frontline practice in a larger system, and the highly institutionalized nature of healthcare settings, to show how actors exercised their agency to engage in workplace processes to promote organizational change. Studies show how actors can use specific institutional logics, strategically use rhetoric, manage emotions, and otherwise engage in purposeful action to change institutions. Other work has taken advantage of the pluralistic character of healthcare contexts to reveal new insights into the arrangement of institutional logics within a field and associated changes in practice.

Future research.   We suggest that healthcare remains an excellent setting to study ongoing questions about institutional change. Although the volume of published articles investigating different aspects of institutional theory is very high, we note that some questions still remain unanswered. There is current interest in gaining a better understanding of micro–meso–macrolevel connections and how they impact processes of institutional change. Healthcare settings are well suited to further investigation of these connections because services are delivered at the front line and, at the same time, embedded in a broader system that typically consists of actors at multiple levels of analysis (organizational, local community, state/province, and national). Learning more about the nature of such connections is important to understand how larger initiatives can move forward, and how they can be derailed.

In addition, scholars are currently curious about the agentic behavior of frontline actors and how they can take local action that transforms into much broader system-level change. For example, the concept of practice-driven institutionalism (Smets et al., 2017) draws on earlier research by scholars such as Selznick (1949) in combination with more recent investigations of practice innovation to reveal new ways of conceptualizing institutional change. Recent attention to the role of emotions and potential connections with institutions also opens up important areas for further research. As institutional researchers turn their attention to people and people's ability to make a difference, there are steadily increasing research opportunities to consider how concepts such as sensemaking and emotions matter to institutional theory.

Consequently, future research in healthcare settings can build on the developing literature to further explore how innovation within highly institutionalized settings can be developed at the front line, and how it can influence the broader system. Researchers could investigate, for example, how collaboration among frontline workers can facilitate macrolevel change. Future research could also take advantage of the frequency of government-led initiatives in healthcare to examine both the processes through which such initiatives are realized and their implementation at the front line. Current global experiences with Covid-19 open up opportunities for researchers to address questions such as: how do emotional responses to a crisis translate into processes of institutional change? Can multiple coexisting institutional logics provide more effective approaches to unexpected disruptions? How can new practices gain legitimacy in a field characterized by crisis? In addition, given the global reach of the Covid-19 pandemic, there will be fertile ground for comparative studies of how different health systems (examples of different institutional fields and their infrastructures) respond to a crisis, and the role of transnational actors, such as the World Health Organization and other macrolevel institutional actors.

4.2 Professions and Organizations

Summary.   Our review of organizational articles showed strong attention to the topic of professionals and how they interact with organizations. Since healthcare contexts are characterized by a highly professionalized workforce, they have provided researchers with an excellent opportunity to examine single professions, relationships between and among different professions, and the ways in which organizations impact professional dynamics. Articles based on healthcare settings have enriched our understanding of how professions change and are maintained, as well as how new professions emerge. Healthcare contexts have also provided fertile ground for improving theory about boundary work among different professional groups.

Future research.   Since professionals increasingly work at least partly inside the boundaries of organizations, we see there is a strong need for further investigations into the relationships between professionals and organizations. Current research has focused on the ways organizations attempt to control professional behavior, but the reverse may also be important. We have some understanding of the ways in which professionals impact organizations, but more is needed. Studies show that organizations may attempt to reduce the rise of new professions, but there are also suggestions that organizations can encourage professionalization. More research is needed to understand these important dynamics.

Societal trends seem to show reducing levels of trust in knowledge held by established professions; instead, we see more reliance on information that is readily available through social media. This erosion of trust can manifest in a number of ways, and we need more research to understand how professions and professionals are impacted. It may be that increasingly serious turf wars among different professionals arise, or we may see a consolidation of professions as a result. Either of these scenarios (or others) deserve close scrutiny because professionals currently play an important role in society; threats to professionalism have the potential to disrupt many aspects of life. We encourage researchers to follow these events over time.

Future research in healthcare contexts can advance theory about professionals by taking account of both long-term trends and environmental shocks. For example, researchers could study how the drive for efficiency in healthcare influences the division of labor between physicians and other professionals. Potential research questions include: under what conditions do physicians delegate work over which they have control to other professionals, such as nurses, or to other occupational groups, such as community health workers? What are the effects of such changes in the control of work for the professional groups involved? As societal trust in professionals is questioned, how do they respond?

Researchers could also consider how the implementation of technology impacts the traditional values of physicians and their relationships with other professionals. For example, artificial intelligence is making significant inroads into medicine. To what extent, if any, do algorithms generated by artificial intelligence complement, or substitute for, decision-making by clinicians? What are the consequences of artificial intelligence for professional autonomy? It would also be interesting to investigate the effects of artificial intelligence on physicians' learning models and whether these new learning models more broadly affect physicians' interactions with each other, and with other health professionals.

In addition, future research should examine how the explosion of telemedicine associated with the Covid-19 pandemic has affected professional work and relationships among professional groups. Research is needed to examine how decisions made by hospitals attempting to adapt to the large influx of Covid-19 patients affected professionals and their work. How have these efforts challenged traditional values of professionals? Are they resulting in new ways of working within and between different professional groups that persist past the crisis (D'Aunno, 2020)? These are critically important questions for the future of professionals – not only in healthcare settings, but also for professionals working in other organizations.

4.3 Social Identity

Summary.   Our review showed that organizational articles based in healthcare contexts have advanced the literature on social identity, particularly with respect to professional identity and role. The highly professionalized workforce that characterizes hospitals and other healthcare organizations has facilitated important research focused on processes of identity change that are tightly connected with the nature of work and the organizational environment. Given the global and multidisciplinary nature of the healthcare workforce, researchers have been able to make strong contributions to theory by showing how international factors and the actions of others can influence processes of identity change.

Future research.   Although there is already a large volume of research on identity and related topics, there continue to be gaps in our knowledge base about how different types of identity, such as professional identity or organizational identity, are altered over time. The continual changes in the healthcare environment, and in society more generally, present many opportunities for researchers to investigate such identity-related topics and advance theory. Since, as we explained earlier, professionals are experiencing eroding levels of public trust, their sense of identity or how they see themselves is also being threatened. New lines of identity research are emerging that have begun to reveal important emotional responses to such threats and how professionals or other groups respond (e.g., Goodrick et al., 2020). However, further research is needed to gain a more complete understanding of different emotional aspects associated with identity and processes of identity change.

We also suggest that other shifts in societal values may impact the identity of professionals and organizations. For example, does the increased interest in population health because of challenges from Covid-19 have implications for how healthcare organizations and professionals see themselves? If so, how are such processes of identity change occurring over time? Researchers could also investigate changes in professional identity arising from the continual drive in healthcare to control costs by using less expensive replacements for physicians. This strategy of employing lowest-cost providers challenges the traditional ways in which healthcare professionals see themselves. For example, when nurses take over work previously provided by physicians, how is professional identity impacted? Are there changes in how physicians and patients view nurses who work with more scope and autonomy than they previously held? How does physician identity change over time as other professionals take over some of their responsibilities?

We also note that changes in healthcare associated with the increasing use of artificial intelligence provide an interesting opportunity to investigate how the identities of physicians and other health professionals change over time. What is the impact on professional identity when tasks are reallocated to a machine?

How does organizational identity change when robotics become an integral component of service delivery?

As a final point related to social identity, we draw attention to recent studies that highlight the importance of understanding "who we are not" as well as "who we are" (e.g., Chreim et al., 2020). When groups or organizations are under threat, it may be possible to better understand counter-identities and the role they play in organizational life. Similarly, established theory about the importance of identity for organizations and teams in times of threat or crisis remains underdeveloped. Healthcare settings provide interesting opportunities for theoretical advancement in these respects.

4.4 Networks

Summary.   The articles we reviewed based in healthcare contexts advanced network theory by showing the importance of network structure, particularly the broker role, for a range of organizational outcomes. Because of the rich data gained from cases situated in healthcare settings, the research in this area has identified important factors that influence the effectiveness of networks. Overall, the research articles we reviewed contribute to network theory by showing that the structure of networks matters, and by showing that the characteristics of network ties and brokers within networks are also critical.

Future research.   We suggest that researchers should build on new conceptualizations of networks that highlight an important distinction between brokerage – individuals who occupy a position in a network that links others who are not connected to each other – vs. brokering – the behaviors that brokers might engage in to influence other individuals with whom they are connected in networks (Halevy et al., 2019). This research reveals that, depending on how they behave, individuals occupying a brokerage role can either promote or hinder positive outcomes for networks. For example, brokers can link disparate sources of information to produce an innovation or novel solution to a problem or, in contrast, brokers can block the exchange of information within a social network or even promote conflict between two or more individuals that they bridge. Similarly, other researchers (e.g., Basov & Brennecke, 2017) are focusing attention on important aspects of networks other than their structure, including their cultures and social processes that they entail.

We suggest that healthcare provides an excellent context for studies that follow up on these insights and topics. For example, many healthcare systems have created roles for a variety of professionals to improve the coordination of services for patients (e.g., hospitalist physicians; nurses designated as "care managers"). These individuals are meant to engage in brokering, thus raising several questions for future research, including: what are the characteristics of individuals and their behavior that make them more or less effective in brokering? Does their effectiveness depend more on the network structures in which they are embedded (e.g., large, less cohesive networks vs. smaller, more cohesive networks) or their individual skills, or, importantly, on some interaction of the two? Does it matter how much professional status the individuals hold? Further, are there cultural characteristics of networks that influence the ability of individuals to effectively engage in brokering? For example, are there networks whose cultures promote the autonomy of individual healthcare providers, perhaps at the expense of brokers and brokering that are established to coordinate services both within and across departments of a healthcare organization?

Finally, we suggest that changes in society both in terms of the availability of communication technology and the persistence of crises provide opportunities for research based in healthcare contexts to improve theory about networks. For example, researchers could consider how networks change in response to crisis. Do the same relationships remain important? How does urgency and the need for speed influence network development? Other research could explore how the availability of new technologies that facilitate nonproximal communication affects the structure and outcomes of networks, including their size and cohesion (Myers, 2020). Do connections based on face-to-face contact strengthen or weaken connections? With the large-scale introduction of new technologies, do networks tend to become larger or smaller than those relying on traditional communication?

4.5 Diffusion of Innovation

Summary.   We found that articles relying on healthcare contexts advanced theory about the diffusion of innovation by focusing on the spread of technical innovations, knowledge transfer from one place to another, and the transfer of knowledge to practice. Studies focusing on the diffusion of technical innovations enriched theory by showing how the organizational and institutional context influenced the way new technologies diffuse. Articles advancing theory about knowledge transfer showed the importance of key actors who are able to modify concepts within their context in ways that alter translation processes. Similarly, those studies focusing on the transfer of knowledge to practice highlight the importance of key organizational agents in the success or failure of processes designed to realize knowledge in practice.

Future research.   Current research on the diffusion of innovation is beginning to move away from previous models that conceptualize the process as one occurring in straight lines. Instead, researchers are explaining the travel of ideas as multidirectional, and more similar to the spread of a virus than travel on an airplane (Rovik, 2011). More research to improve our understanding of such nonlinear processes is very much needed. The current literature is well established in terms of tracing the uptake and implementation of new technology, but gaps in our knowledge remain regarding variation in the speed of such uptake, and the resulting impact on practice patterns.

Future research based in healthcare settings could investigate the current proliferation of technological developments in many aspects of service provision. For example, the practice of medicine is increasingly reliant on artificial intelligence (Eaneff, Obermeyer, & Butte, 2020). How is the spread of artificial intelligence similar to or different from other technical advances? How can the creation of positions (such as organizational knowledge brokers) dedicated to advancing the transfer of knowledge to practice influence the adoption of innovations (Nguyen et al., 2020)? Researchers should also take advantage of healthcare fields' inherent complexity by studying the dynamics of diffusion in fragmented fields. How well do our established conceptual models account for the spread of innovations in fields that involve multiple and inconsistent logics, a variety of professional groups vying for influence, and government policies crossing levels of jurisdiction? Similarly, future research could focus on the contagion-like spread of some ideas, while other seemingly good ideas are ignored. The context of healthcare provides variability across countries and across sectors that facilitates the examination of similarities and differences in how technology, ideas, or practices travel (or not). Further studies of these processes and differences in how innovations originate are likely to reveal new understandings that can be relevant in many other settings.

4.6 Organizational Change

Summary.   Although the volume of research investigating organizational change is very large, we still need to develop a better understanding of why so many change initiatives do not succeed. Organizational researchers have responded by investigating different aspects of organizational change in healthcare settings, attempting to provide theoretical explanations for success or failure. Some studies have taken a process approach, engaging in micro- and mesolevel analyses to explain how different ways of collaborating, coordinating, or interacting can lead to organizational change. Other studies have focused attention at the organizational level, explaining how restructuring or redesigning work can impact organizational change initiatives. We also identified a third category of research showing how organizational processes or outcomes can be improved through change initiatives. Finally, we showed that some researchers have taken a more innovative approach by investigating how processes of sensemaking can impact change in organizations. Overall, we see that research on organizational change in healthcare settings has taken multiple lines of sight, attempting to provide better answers about how desired organizational change can be realized.

Future *research*.   The different approaches that researchers have used to examine organizational change, and the mixed results that these studies have produced, suggest that a relatively large number of varied factors affect the extent to which organizations change, the nature of change, and the success of planned change projects. Given this state of knowledge, healthcare settings may be particularly useful empirical contexts to continue to advance understanding of organizational change because their complexity allows researchers to examine a variety of alternative explanations. For example, researchers can use healthcare settings to conceptualize how institutional forces and market pressure for increased efficiency affect organizational change, taking into account the roles that professionals, including their networks and social identities, play in promoting or resisting change programs.

In addition, we encourage researchers to continue investigating organizational change from multiple points of view. With increased attention to the role of emotion, research questions could include: how do the emotional responses of frontline providers influence motivation and engagement in change initiatives? When surgeons must learn new skills by practicing on simulators (as shown by Beane, 2019), how is their fundamental relationship with patients altered, and do organizational work processes change as a result? The impact of Covid-19 also provides many opportunities for studying organizational change. Researchers could study how hospitals have quickly adapted to new requirements for safety protocols, including protective equipment and more complicated triaging processes. In response to the pandemic, healthcare organizations throughout the world have found ways to work together, sharing best evidence with respect to safety protocols, public health regulations, and vaccine development. Will these new collaborative arrangements lead to sustainable change in working relationships? Or will organizations return to their more competitive relationships? We see that the multifaceted and ongoing ways in which healthcare organizations engage in change initiatives will continue to provide researchers with excellent research settings for years to come.

4.7 Connecting Organization Theory and Healthcare Research

Turning now to research focused on the provision of healthcare services, we observed that healthcare researchers have increased their interest in studying organization and management, as opposed to focusing solely on clinical or policy issues. This presents an opportunity for increasing use of organization theory to inform healthcare research. Indeed, an important aim of this Element is to encourage healthcare researchers to more purposefully employ organization theory in ways that help to advance knowledge about the provision of healthcare services. We argue that theory-informed healthcare research can produce important insights for managers, policy-makers, and clinicians that otherwise may have been overlooked. As Figure 2 illustrates, we see that organization theory and healthcare research should be more tightly connected. Organization theory can improve healthcare research by guiding the construction of hypotheses and the interpretation of data to develop practical knowledge about, for example, improving access to and the quality and cost of healthcare services. In turn, findings from healthcare research can help to inform organization theory by posing theoretical puzzles in response to unanswered empirical questions and findings that are contrary to established theory.

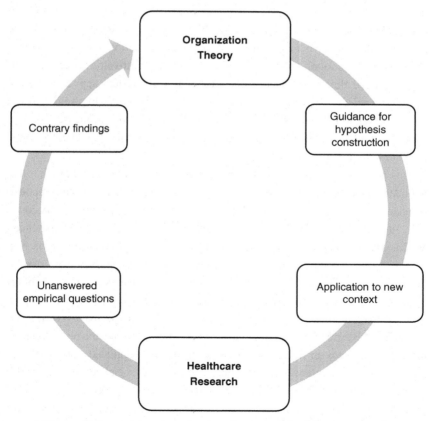

Figure 2 Connecting organization theory and healthcare research

However, as we showed in Section 3, our review of articles in leading healthcare management journals revealed that theory did not figure as prominently as we had initially expected. We also found that the theories drawn upon in healthcare journals did not consistently match those dominating the organization theory journals. While we found that researchers drew on institutional theory and organizational change approaches, we also saw that some of the theories guiding healthcare management research, such as resource dependence and transaction cost theory, did not figure prominently in the organization theory journals.

The connections, or rather the lack thereof, we observed between the theories prevalent in organization theory journals compared to healthcare management journals can be viewed as reflecting both strengths and weaknesses of both literatures. An important strength of organization theory journals is their focus on the rigorous development of theory in an increasingly broad variety of contexts as opposed to only business organizations. At the same time, we observe an increasing focus in organization theory journals on valuing interesting or surprising findings, as opposed to the more incremental accumulation of knowledge. The use of theories in the healthcare management literature, which presently do not have much currency in the organization theory literature, reflects organizational theorists' preoccupation with novelty. It seems that organizational theorists tend to lose interest in a theoretical approach before examining all the important and unanswered questions. As Figure 2 shows, unanswered empirical questions and contrary findings from healthcare research ideally should enrich the development of organization theory. We do not see this happening to any great extent.

This partly reflects a lack of interest in replication or in specifying what the boundary conditions of theories might be. It also reflects the fact that practical applications are not particularly valued by the leading organization theory journals, despite the often-obligatory paragraphs on implications for practice. Healthcare researchers are more focused on practice, and if theoretical approaches are developed in settings outside of healthcare, they are particularly interested in the extent to which such theories are relevant for a healthcare setting. As we have observed in our review, they may not even be interested when theory is developed in healthcare settings, but not published in healthcare journals. Healthcare researchers also are interested in scope. If theory explains a specific phenomenon, there is a tendency in healthcare to be skeptical of its application to a related phenomenon. In contrast, organizational theorists are socialized into a world where contribution to theory requires a strong degree of novelty, or else a study is likely to be categorized as "just another study on x" and therefore not worthy of publication.

One of the strengths of research published in healthcare journals is that it is framed in ways that enable the results to be used to inform practice and develop practice. On the other hand, sometimes healthcare researchers seem to be only focused on empirics without guidance from current organization theory to suggest what is important. Healthcare researchers can also remain attached to familiar theories without considering whether there are theoretical developments that may provide additional insight. We found that even when healthcare researchers were drawing on theories currently in play in organization theory journals, their arguments were sometimes based on much older publications. While core principles of theory can be enshrined in classic work, additional insights for practice and policy could be gained by building on current developments in theory.

In sum, we observe that the lack of connection between research in organization theory and research in healthcare can be at least partially explained by the realization that these two groups seem to be addressing different questions. Healthcare researchers are interested in assessing organizational outcomes and performance, particularly, as noted earlier, from the perspective of quality, cost, and access to services. For example, healthcare researchers often examine the organizational outcomes of new policy initiatives such as new payment systems to improve the cost and quality of care. In contrast, researchers in organization theory are often more interested in processes (e.g., how does organizational change occur in response to particular policy initiatives?) and intermediate outcomes (e.g., did an organization develop a specialized unit or roles to respond to a new policy?). From an institutional theory perspective, researchers may be interested in whether organizations are becoming more similar or are changing in response to a new policy, while healthcare researchers would reply by asking, "So what if organizations are changing or becoming more alike: what patient outcomes or costs do organizational changes produce?"

We argue not only that both approaches and sets of questions are important, but also that what we now need are more studies that simultaneously focus on both organizational processes and outcomes. Outcome studies that pay little attention to the processes involved in change cannot develop a better understanding of how to achieve the desired ends. Similarly, studies of organizational processes that do not consider outcomes are also suboptimal because they leave us with little information about how to improve clinical and organizational performance. In short, researchers in both groups can increase their impact by combining their expertise and perspectives.

Further, if organizational researchers focus more of their attention on organizational outcomes, they would open up better opportunities for increasing the impact of their work. In addition, they could then more easily follow the lead of healthcare researchers who commonly use social media, press releases, blogs, and videos to show how their results are meaningful for policy-makers, managers, and clinicians. We recognize that, for many organizational researchers who are focused on theory-building, these steps would require time and effort; but we maintain that they could fruitfully improve the impact of such work.

To improve both organization theory and healthcare research, we suggest that attention to the boxes identified in Figure 2 could facilitate much stronger connections between organization theory and healthcare research. We encourage healthcare researchers to consistently examine new developments in organization theory, particularly when new conceptual perspectives or concepts are developed through research conducted in healthcare settings. Such attention can provide important guidance for designing new research projects, including for developing hypotheses and focusing on particular aspects of organizational contexts. In addition, we encourage healthcare researchers to apply newly developed theory to a variety of healthcare contexts. Theory should be tested across different segments of healthcare (e.g., acute care, long-term care, mental health, and systems in a variety of nations) to determine boundary conditions and limits to applicability.

We also call for action on the part of organization theorists. In developing new research projects, it is critical to consider not only existing theory but also the results of previous empirical healthcare research. For example, when healthcare researchers apply theory to new contexts, organizational theorists should pay attention to unanswered empirical questions that arise. In addition, healthcare research can result in findings that are contrary to theory-based predictions. These puzzling empirical findings should be closely examined by organization theorists, and used to develop new studies that help to improve theory over time. We believe that it is through such interconnected activities of healthcare researchers and organization theorists that important knowledge can be advanced.

Thus, we join the voices of others who are advocating for stronger connections among researchers whose main aim, on the one hand, is to promote organization theory and those who aim, on the other hand, to promote advanced in the practice of healthcare across clinical, management, and policy domains. Indeed, we can point to several mechanisms that are already in place to move in this direction. These include:

(1) *joint training programs for doctoral students*, as is done, for example, in the Doctoral Program in Organizational Behavior at Harvard University, which includes students from healthcare, business, sociology, and other disciplines;

(2) *symposia, workshops, and panels jointly sponsored by academic organizations such as the Academy of Management Divisions*, especially ones that link the division of Healthcare Management to other relevant divisions such as Organization and Management Theory, Organizational Behavior, and Strategic Management;

(3) *special issues of journals (or special journals)* that focus on building connections between theory and practice (such as the *Medical Research and Review* Special Issue of 2016 on Accountable Care Organizations and Organizational Theory, and the relatively new journal *BMJ Leader*);

(4) *bridge-building between organizational researchers and researchers in the growing field of implementation science* (Birken et al., 2017; Nilsen & Birken, 2020). Research in implementation science focuses explicitly on ways to promote organizational change in the healthcare field, with particular attention on increasing the use of evidence-based practices among healthcare providers;

(5) *small-scale, focused conferences* that bring together diverse stakeholders, including practitioners and researchers who specialize in healthcare and organizational studies.

One of the present authors (Tom D'Aunno) can attest to the influence that a focused conference had on his research. In September 1984, he participated in a small conference that boosted his interest in strengthening ties between practice-focused research and organization theory. W. R. (Dick) Scott and Ken Lutterman, the Associate Director for Mental Health Services Planning and Research at the National Institute of Mental Health, organized the conference, which brought together organization theorists, researchers studying mental health agencies and systems, managers of state mental health systems, and researchers. John Meyer and Dick Scott each presented a paper that used institutional theory to analyze the organization of mental health services (the conference papers are available in the *American Behavioral Scientist*, 1986 (28), 5) (Meyer, 1985; Scott & Black, 1985).

This work inspired Tom to draw on institutional theory in a national study of community mental health centers and drug abuse treatment programs that he was conducting, and resulted in his 1991 article in the *Academy of Management Journal* titled "Isomorphism and external support in conflicting institutional environments: A study of drug abuse treatment units" (coauthored with his mentor, Richard Price, and Robert I. Sutton) (D'Aunno, Sutton, & Price, 1991). This was one of the first papers to advance understanding of organizational responses to institutional environments characterized by multiple, inconsistent logics – a line of research that became one of the most central and robust in institutional theory. This paper also helped to advance practice and policy by uncovering key mechanisms through which clients with mental health and substance use disorders can receive treatment that is not evidence-based – a problem that remains ongoing and that calls for more organizational research.

4.8 Our Final Words

In concluding this Element, we make a few overall observations and an appeal. Our review of articles in organization journals revealed a growing prevalence of research conducted in healthcare settings, and showed how various aspects of healthcare provide excellent opportunities for developing theoretical contributions. In reviewing the use of these theoretical advancements in healthcare management journals, we found that there were far fewer direct linkages than we had anticipated. In some ways we realize this should not be surprising, since many aspects of academia (and modern society) have become increasingly specialized over time, resulting in relatively small enclaves of researchers who converse mostly with each other. However, we propose that in contrast to this phenomenon of increasing specialization, significantly more bidirectional travel of research ideas between organization theory and healthcare management research could be beneficial to both sides. The important questions in healthcare today are multifaceted, requiring thoughtful attention by multiple types of experts. We hope that our ideas here might help to encourage researchers to reach across academic boundaries as they continue striving to improve knowledge.

References

Abbott, A. (1988). *The System of Professions: An Essay on the Division of Expert Labor*. Chicago: The University of Chicago Press.

Adler, P. S., & Kwon, S.-W. (2013). The mutation of professionalism as a contested diffusion process: Clinical guidelines as carriers of institutional change in medicine. *Journal of Management Studies*, 50(5): 930–962.

Alvesson, M., & Blom, M. (2018). Beyond leadership and followership: Working with a variety of modes of organizing. *Organizational Dynamics*, 48(1): 28–37.

Alvesson, M., & Willmott, H. (2002). Identity regulation as organizational control: Producing the appropriate individual. *Journal of Management Studies*, 39(5): 619–644.

Alvesson, M., Lee Ashcraft, K., & Thomas, R. (2008). Identity matters: Reflections on the construction of identity scholarship in organization studies. *Organization*, 15(1): 5–28.

Ansari, S. M., Fiss, P. C., & Zajac, E. J. (2010). Made to fit: How practices vary as they diffuse. *Academy of Management Review*, 35(1): 67–92.

Antino, M., Rico, R., & Thatcher, S. M. B. (2019). Structuring reality through the faultlines lens: The effects of structure, fairness, and status conflict on the activated faultlines–performance relationship. *Academy of Management Journal*, 62(5): 1444–1470.

Aristidou, A., & Barrett, M. (2018). Coordinating service provision in dynamic service settings: A position-practice relations perspective. *Academy of Management Journal*, 61(2): 685–714.

Ashforth, B. E., & Mael, F. (1989). Social identity theory and the organization. *Academy of Management Review*, 14(1): 20–39.

Barrett, M., Oborn, E., Orlikowski, W. J., & Yates, J. (2012). Reconfiguring boundary relations: Robotic innovations in pharmacy work. *Organization Science*, 23(5): 1448–1466.

Basov, N., & Brennecke, J. (2017). Duality beyond dyads: Multiplex patterning of social ties and cultural meanings. *Research in the Sociology of Organizations*, 53: 87–112.

Battilana, J. (2011). The enabling role of social position in diverging from the institutional status quo: Evidence from the UK national health service. *Organization Science*, 22(4): 817–834.

Battilana, J., & Casciaro, T. (2012). Change agents, networks, and institutions: A contingency theory of organizational change. *Academy of Management Journal*, 55(2): 381–398.

Beane, M. (2019). Shadow learning: Building robotic surgical skill when approved means fail. *Administrative Science Quarterly*, 64(1): 87–123.

Berghout, M. A., Oldenhof, L., Fabbricotti, I. N., & Hilders, C. G. J. M. (2018). Discursively framing physicians as leaders: Institutional work to reconfigure medical professionalism. *Social Science & Medicine*, 212: 68–75.

Birken, S. A., Powell, B. J., Shea, C. M., Haines, E. R., Alexis Kirk, M., Leeman, J., Rohweder, C., Damschroder, L., & Presseau, J. (2017). Criteria for selecting implementation science theories and frameworks: Results from an international survey. *Implementation Science*, 12(1): 124.

Borgatti, S. P., & Ofem, B. (2010). Social network theory and analysis. In A. Daly (Ed.), *Social Network Theory and Educational Change* (17–29). Cambridge, MA: Harvard Education Press.

Bucher, S. V., Chreim, S., Langley, A., & Reay, T. (2016). Contestation about collaboration: Discursive boundary work among professions. *Organization Studies*, 37(4): 497–522.

Burrage, M., & Torstendahl, R. (1990). *Professions in Theory and History: Rethinking the Study of the Professions*. London: Sage.

Burt, R. (1992). *Structural Holes: The Social Structure of Competition*. Cambridge, MA: Harvard University Press.

Burt, R. S., Kilduff, M., & Tasselli, S. (2013). Social network analysis: Foundations and frontiers on advantage. *Annual Review of Psychology*, 64(1): 527–547.

Caldwell, N. D., Roehrich, J. K., & George, G. (2017). Social value creation and relational coordination in public-private collaborations. *Journal of Management Studies*, 54(6): 906–928.

Cappellaro, G., Tracey, P., & Greenwood, R. (2020). From logic acceptance to logic rejection: The process of destabilization in hybrid organizations. *Organization Science*, 31(2): 415–438.

Carr-Saunders, A. M., & Wilson, P. A. (1933). *The Professions*. Oxford: Clarendon Press.

Chown, J. (2020). Financial incentives and professionals' work tasks: The moderating effects of jurisdictional dominance and prominence. *Organization Science*, 31(4): 887–908.

Chreim, S., Williams, B. E., & Hinings, C. R. (2007). Interlevel influences on the reconstruction of professional role identity. *Academy of Management Journal*, 50(6): 1515–1539.

Chreim, S., Langley, A., Reay, T., Comeau-Vallée, M., & Huq, J.-L. (2020). Constructing and sustaining counter-institutional identities. *Academy of Management Journal*, 63(3): 935–964.

Christianson, M. K. (2019). More and less effective updating: The role of trajectory management in making sense again. *Administrative Science Quarterly*, 64(1): 45–86.

Clark, J. R., Huckman, R. S., & Staats, B. R. (2013). Learning from customers: Individual and organizational effects in outsourced radiological services. *Organization Science*, 24(5): 1539–1557.

Coase, R. H. (1937). The nature of the firm. *Economica*, 4(16): 386–405.

Coleman, J., Katz, E., & Menzel, H. (1957). The diffusion of an innovation among physicians. *Sociometry*, 20(4): 253–270.

Compagni, A., Mele, V., & Ravasi, D. (2014). How early implementations influence later adoptions of innovation: Social positioning and skill reproduction in the diffusion of robotic surgery. *Academy of Management Journal*, 58(1): 242–278.

Croft, C., Currie, G., & Lockett, A. (2015). The impact of emotionally important social identities on the construction of a managerial leader identity: A challenge for nurses in the English National Health Service. *Organization Studies*, 36(1): 113–131.

Currie, G., & Spyridonidis, D. (2015). Interpretation of multiple institutional logics on the ground: Actors' position, their agency and situational constraints in professionalized contexts. *Organization Studies*, 37(1): 77–97.

Currie, G., & White, L. (2012). Inter-professional barriers and knowledge brokering in an organizational context: The case of healthcare. *Organization Studies*, 33(10): 1333–1361.

Currie, G., Finn, R., & Martin, G. (2010). Role transition and the interaction of relational and social identity: New nursing roles in the English NHS. *Organization Studies*, 31(7): 941–961.

Currie, G., Lockett, A., Finn, R., Martin, G., & Waring, J. (2012). Institutional work to maintain professional power: Recreating the model of medical professionalism. *Organization Studies*, 33(7): 937–962.

Cuypers, I., Hennart, J.-F., Silverman, B., & Ertug, G. (2020). Transaction cost theory: Past progress, current challenges, and suggestions for the future. *Academy of Management Annals*, 15(1). https://doi.org/10.5465/annals.2019.0051.

Czarniawska, B., & Joerges, B. (1995). Winds of organizational change: How ideas translate into objects and actions. *Research in the Sociology of Organizations*, 13: 171–209.

D'Andreta, D., Marabelli, M., Newell, S., Scarbrough, H., & Swan, J. (2016). Dominant cognitive frames and the innovative power of social networks. *Organization Studies*, 37(3): 293–321.

Dattée, B., & Barlow, J. (2017). Multilevel organizational adaptation: Scale invariance in the Scottish healthcare system. *Organization Science*, 28(2): 301–319.

D'Aunno, T. (2020). Lessons from New York City's response to the coronavirus pandemic. *Mecosan*, 113: 309–312.

D'Aunno, T., Sutton, R. I., & Price, R. H. (1991). Isomorphism and external support in conflicting institutional environments: A study of drug abuse treatment units. *Academy of Management Journal*, 34(3): 636–661.

Davis, G. F., & Cobb, J. A. (2010). Resource dependence theory: Past and future. In S. Claudia Bird & D. Frank (Eds.), *Stanford's Organization Theory Renaissance, 1970–2000* (Vol. 28, 21–42). Bingley: Emerald Group Publishing Limited.

de Bree, M., & Stoopendaal, A. (2018). De- and recoupling and public regulation. *Organization Studies*, 41(5): 599–620.

de Rond, M., & Lok, J. (2016). Some things can never be unseen: The role of context in psychological injury at war. *Academy of Management Journal*, 59(6): 1965–1993.

Desai, V. (2014). Learning through the distribution of failures within an organization: Evidence from heart bypass surgery performance. *Academy of Management Journal*, 58(4): 1032–1050.

Desai, V. M. (2020). Can busy organizations learn to get better? Distinguishing between the competing effects of constrained capacity on the organizational learning process. *Organization Science*, 31(1): 67–84.

Dess, G. G., & Beard, D. W. (1984). Dimensions of organizational task environments. *Administrative Science Quarterly*, 29(1): 52–73.

DiBenigno, J. (2018). Anchored personalization in managing goal conflict between professional groups: The case of U.S. Army mental health care. *Administrative Science Quarterly*, 63(3): 526–569.

DiBenigno, J., & Kellogg, K. C. (2014). Beyond occupational differences: The importance of cross-cutting demographics and dyadic toolkits for collaboration in a U.S. hospital. *Administrative Science Quarterly*, 59(3): 375–408.

Dierynck, B., Leroy, H., Savage, G. T., & Choi, E. (2016). The role of individual and collective mindfulness in promoting occupational safety in health care. *Medical Care Research and Review*, 74(1): 79–96.

Dimaggio, P. (1988). Interest and agency in institutional theory. In L. Zucker (Ed.), *Institutional Patterns and Organizations: Culture and Environment* (3–21). Pensacola, FL: Ballinger Publishing.

DiMaggio, P. J., & Powell, W. W. (1983). The iron cage revisited: Institutional isomorphism and collective rationality in organizational fields. *American Sociological Review*, 48(2): 147–160.

Dupret, K. (2018). Performative silences: Potentiality of organizational change. *Organization Studies*, 40(5): 681–703.

Durkheim, É. (1957). *Professional Ethics and Civic Morals.* London: Routledge & Kegan Paul.

Eaneff, S., Obermeyer, Z., & Butte, A. J. (2020). The case for algorithmic stewardship for artificial intelligence and machine learning technologies. *Jama*, 324(14): 1397–1398.

Edmondson, A. (1999). Psychological safety and learning behavior in work teams. *Administrative Science Quarterly*, 44(2): 350–383.

Emerson, R. M. (1962). Power-dependence relations. *American Sociological Review*, 27(1): 31–41.

Fareed, N., & Mick, S. S. (2011). To make or buy patient safety solutions: A resource dependence and transaction cost economics perspective. *Health Care Management Review*, 36(4): 288–298.

Fareed, N., Bazzoli, G. J., Farnsworth Mick, S. S., & Harless, D. W. (2015). The influence of institutional pressures on hospital electronic health record presence. *Social Science & Medicine*, 133: 28–35.

Ferlie, E., Fitzgerald, L., Wood, M., & Hawkins, C. (2005).The nonspread of innovations: The mediating role of professionals. *Academy of Management Journal*, 48(1): 117–134.

Feyereisen, S., Brochek, J., & Goodrick, E. (2018). Understanding professional jurisdiction changes in the field of anesthesiology. *Medical Care Research and Review*, 74: 612–632.

Finn, R., Currie, G., & Martin, G. (2010). Team work in context: Institutional mediation in the public-service professional bureaucracy. *Organization Studies*, 31(8): 1069–1097.

Freidson, E. (1970). *Professional Dominance: The Social Structure of Medical Care.* New York: Routledge.

Freidson, E. (2001). *Professionalism, the Third Logic: On the Practice of Knowledge.* Chicago: University of Chicago Press.

Friedland, R., & Alford, R. R. (1991). Bringing society back in: Symbols, practices, and institutional contradictions. In W. W. Powell & P. J. DiMaggio (Eds.), *The New Institutionalism in Organizational Analysis* (232–263). Chicago: University of Chicago Press.

Galperin, R. V. (2020). Organizational powers: Contested innovation and loss of professional jurisdiction in the case of retail medicine. *Organization Science*, 31(2): 508–534.

Gardner, J. W., Boyer, K. K., & Ward, P. T. (2017). Achieving time-sensitive organizational performance through mindful use of technologies and routines. *Organization Science*, 28(6): 1061–1079.

Gieryn, T. F. (1983). Boundary-work and the demarcation of science from non-science: Strains and interests in professional ideologies of scientists. *American Sociological Review*, 48(6): 781–795.

Gieryn, T. F. (1999). *Cultural Boundaries of Science: Credibility on the Line.* Chicago: University of Chicago Press.

Gittell, J. H. (2002a). Coordinating mechanisms in care provider groups: Relational coordination as a mediator and input uncertainty as a moderator of performance effects. *Management Science*, 48(11): 1408–1426.

Gittell, J. H. (2002b). Relationships between service providers and their impact on customers. *Journal of Service Research*, 4(4): 299–311.

Goodrick, E., & Reay, T. (2010). Florence Nightingale endures: Legitimizing a new professional role identity. *Journal of Management Studies*, 47(1): 55–84.

Goodrick, E., & Reay, T. (2011). Constellations of institutional logics: Changes in the professional work of pharmacists. *Work and Occupations*, 38(3): 372–416.

Goodrick, E., & Reay, T. (2016). An institutional perspective on account-able care organizations. *Medical Care Research and Review*, 73(6): 685–693.

Goodrick, E., Jarvis, L. C., & Reay, T. (2020). Preserving a professional institution: Emotion in discursive institutional work. *Journal of Management Studies*, 57(4): 735–774.

Gray, C. S., Berta, W., Deber, R., & Lum, J. (2017). Organizational responses to accountability requirements: Do we get what we expect? *Health Care Management Review*, 42(1): 65–75.

Greenwood, B. N., Agarwal, R., Agarwal, R., & Gopal, A. (2019). The role of individual and organizational expertise in the adoption of new practices. *Organization Science*, 30(1): 191–213.

Greenwood, R., Oliver, C., Lawrence, T. B., & Meyer, R. E. (2017). *The Sage Handbook of Organizational Institutionalism* (2nd ed.). London and Thousand Oaks, CA: Sage.

Greenwood, R., Oliver, C., Suddaby, R., & Sahlin-Andersson, K. (2008). *The Sage Handbook of Organizational Institutionalism* (1st ed.). London and Thousand Oaks, CA: Sage.

Greenwood, R., Raynard, M., Kodeih, F., Micelotta, E. R., & Lounsbury, M. (2011). Institutional complexity and organizational responses. *Academy of Management Annals*, 5(1): 317–371.

Gupta, B., & Khanna, T. (2019). A recombination-based internationalization model: Evidence from Narayana health's journey from India to the Cayman Islands. *Organization Science*, 30(2): 405–425.

Halevy, N., Halali, E., & Zlatev, J. J. (2019). Brokerage and brokering: An integrative review and organizing framework for third party influence. *Academy of Management Annals*, 13(1): 215–239.

Heaphy, E. D. (2017). "Dancing on hot coals": How emotion work facilitates collective sensemaking. *Academy of Management Journal*, 60(2): 642–670.

Heinze, K. L., & Weber, K. (2016). Toward organizational pluralism: Institutional intrapreneurship in integrative medicine. *Organization Science*, 27(1): 157–172.

Herepath, A., & Kitchener, M. (2016). When small bandages fail: The field-level repair of severe and protracted institutional breaches. *Organization Studies*, 37(8): 1113–1139.

Hesse, J., Krishnan, R., & Moers, F. (2016). Selective regulator decoupling and organizations' strategic responses. *Academy of Management Journal*, 59(6): 2178–2204.

Heugens, P. P. M. A. R., & Lander, M. W. (2009). Structure! Agency! (and other quarrels): A meta-analysis of institutional theories of organization. *Academy of Management Journal*, 52(1): 61–85.

Hsieh, H.-M., Clement, D. G., & Bazzoli, G. J. (2010). Impacts of market and organizational characteristics on hospital efficiency and uncompensated care. *Health Care Management Review*, 35(1): 77–87.

Huber, T. P., Rodriguez, H. P., & Shortell, S. M. (2020). The influence of leadership facilitation on relational coordination among primary care team members of accountable care organizations. *Health Care Management Review*, 45 (4): 302–310.

Jay, J. (2013). Navigating paradox as a mechanism of change and innovation in hybrid organizations. *Academy of Management Journal*, 56(1): 137–159.

Jung, O. S., Blasco, A., & Lakhani, K. R. (2020). Innovation contest: Effect of perceived support for learning on participation. *Health Care Management Review*, 45(3): 255–266.

Kellogg, Katherine C. (2009). Operating room: Relational spaces and micro-institutional change in surgery. *American Journal of Sociology*, 115(3): 657–711.

Kellogg, K. C. (2011). Hot lights and cold steel: Cultural and political toolkits for practice change in surgery. *Organization Science*, 22(2): 482–502.

Kellogg, K. C. (2012). Making the cut: Using status-based countertactics to block social movement implementation and microinstitutional change in surgery. *Organization Science*, 23(6): 1546–1570.

Kellogg, K. C. (2018). Subordinate activation tactics: Semi-professionals and micro-level institutional change in professional organizations. *Administrative Science Quarterly*, 64(4): 928–975.

Kennedy, M. T., & Fiss, P. C. (2009). Institutionalization, framing, and diffusion: The logic of TQM adoption and implementation decisions among U.S. hospitals. *Academy of Management Journal*, 52(5): 897–918.

Kern, A., Laguecir, A., & Leca, B. (2017). Behind smoke and mirrors: A political approach to decoupling. *Organization Studies*, 39(4): 543–564.

King, E. B., Dawson, J. F., West, M. A., Gilrane, V. L., Peddie, C. I., & Bastin, L. (2011). Why organizational and community diversity matter: Representativeness and the emergence of incivility and organizational performance. *Academy of Management Journal*, 54(6): 1103–1118.

Kislov, R., Hyde, P., & McDonald, R. (2017). New game, old rules? Mechanisms and consequences of legitimation in boundary spanning activities. *Organization Studies*, 38(10): 1421–1444.

Kraatz, M. S. (2020). Boundaries, bridges and brands: A comment on Alvesson, Hallett, and Spicer's "uninhibited institutionalisms." *Journal of Management Inquiry*, 29(3): 254–261.

Kraatz, M. S., & Block, E. S. (2008). Organizational implications of institutional pluralism. In R. Greenwood, C. Oliver, R. Suddaby, & K. Sahlin (Eds.), *The Sage Handbook of Organizational Institutionalism* (243–275). London: Sage.

Kyratsis, Y., Atun, R., Phillips, N., Tracey, P., & George, G. (2017). Health systems in transition: Professional identity work in the context of shifting institutional logics. *Academy of Management Journal*, 60(2): 610–641.

Larson, M. S. (1977). *The Rise of Professionalism: A Sociological Analysis*. Berkeley, CA: University of California Press.

Lawrence, T. B. (2017). High-stakes institutional translation: Establishing North America's first government-sanctioned supervised injection site. *Academy of Management Journal*, 60(5): 1771–1800.

Lawrence, T. B., & Suddaby, R. (2006). Institutions and institutional work. In S. R. Clegg, C. Hardy, T. B. Lawrence, & W. R. Nord (Eds.), *The Sage Handbook of Organization Studies* (215–254). London: Sage.

Lawrence, T. B., Suddaby, R., & Leca, B. (2009). Introduction: Theorizing and studying institutional work. In *Institutional Work: Actors and Agency in Institutional Studies of Organizations* (1–28). Cambridge: Cambridge University Press.

Lewin, K. (1951). *Field Theory in Social Science*. New York: Harper & Row.

Lockett, A., Currie, G., Finn, R., Martin, G., & Waring, J. (2013). The influence of social position on sensemaking about organizational change. *Academy of Management Journal*, 57(4): 1102–1129.

Macfarlane, F., Barton-Sweeney, C., Woodard, F., & Greenhalgh, T. (2013). Achieving and sustaining profound institutional change in healthcare: Case study using neo-institutional theory. *Social Science & Medicine*, 80: 10–18.

Maltarich, M. A., Nyberg, A. J., Reilly, G., Abdulsalam, D. D., & Martin, M. (2017). Pay-for-performance, sometimes: An interdisciplinary approach to integrating economic rationality with psychological emotion to predict individual performance. *Academy of Management Journal*, 60(6): 2155–2174.

Martin, G., Currie, G., Weaver, S., Finn, R., & McDonald, R. (2016). Institutional complexity and individual responses: Delineating the boundaries of partial autonomy. *Organization Studies*, 38(1): 103–127.

McCann, L., Granter, E., Hyde, P., & Hassard, J. (2013). Still blue-collar after all these years? An ethnography of the professionalization of emergency ambulance work. *Journal of Management Studies*, 50(5): 750–776.

McGivern, G., Dopson, S., Ferlie, E., Fischer, M., Fitzgerald, L., Ledger, J., & Bennett, C. (2017). The silent politics of temporal work: A case study of a management consultancy project to redesign public health care. *Organization Studies*, 39(8): 1007–1030.

Menachemi, N., & Collum, T. H. (2011). Benefits and drawbacks of electronic health record systems. *Risk Management and Healthcare Policy*, 4: 47–55.

Menachemi, N., Mazurenko, O., Kazley, A. S., Diana, M. L., & Ford, E. W. (2012). Market factors and electronic medical record adoption in medical practices. *Health Care Manage Rev*, 37(1): 14–22.

Meyer, J. W. (1985). Institutional and organizational rationalization in the mental health system. *American Behavioral Scientist*, 28(5): 587–600.

Meyer, J. W., & Rowan, B. (1978). *The Structure of Educational Organizations*. San Francisco, CA: Jossey-Bass.

Mick, S. S. F., & Shay, P. D. (2016). Accountable care organizations and transaction cost economics. *Medical Care Research and Review*, 73(6): 649–659.

Muzio, D., Aulakh, S., & Kirkpatrick, I. (2019). *Professional Occupations and Organizations*. Cambridge: Cambridge University Press.

Muzio, D., Brock, D. M., & Suddaby, R. (2013). Professions and institutional change: Towards an institutionalist sociology of the professions. *Journal of Management Studies*, 50(5): 699–721.

Myers, C. G. (2020). Vicarious learning in the time of coronavirus. *Behavioral Science & Policy*, 5(2). https://issuu.com/behavioralsciencepolicyassocia tion/docs/bsp.

Nancarrow, S. A., & Borthwick, A. M. (2005). Dynamic professional boundaries in the healthcare workforce. *Sociology of Health & Illness*, 27(7): 897–919.

Nembhard, I. M., & Tucker, A. L. (2011). Deliberate learning to improve performance in dynamic service settings: Evidence from hospital intensive care units. *Organization Science*, 22(4): 907–922.

Nguyen, A. M., Cuthel, A., Padgett, D. K., Niles, P., Rogers, E., Pham-Singer, H., ... Shelley, D. (2020). How practice facilitation strategies differ by practice context. *Journal of General Internal Medicine*, 35(3): 824–831.

Nigam, A., & Dokko, G. (2019). Career resourcing and the process of professional emergence. *Academy of Management Journal*, 62(4): 1052–1084.

Nigam, A., & Ocasio, W. (2010). Event attention, environmental sensemaking, and change in institutional logics: An inductive analysis of the effects of public attention to Clinton's health care reform initiative. *Organization Science*, 21(4): 823–841.

Nigam, A., Huising, R., & Golden, B. (2016). Explaining the selection of routines for change during organizational search. *Administrative Science Quarterly*, 61(4): 551–583.

Nilsen, P., & Birken, S. A. (2020). *Handbook on Implementation Science*. Cheltenham: Edward Elgar Publishing.

Ocasio, W., & Gai, S. L. (2020). Institutions: Everywhere but not everything. *Journal of Management Inquiry*, 29(3): 262–271.

Oliver, C. (1991). Strategic responses to institutional processes. *Academy of Management Review*, 16(1): 145–179.

Pahnke, E. C., Katila, R., & Eisenhardt, K. M. (2015). Who takes you to the dance? How partners' institutional logics influence innovation in young firms. *Administrative Science Quarterly*, 60(4): 596–633.

Parsons, T. (1951). *The Social System*. Glencoe, IL: Free Press.

Pfeffer, J., & Salancik, G. R. (1978). *The External Control of Organizations: A Resource Dependence Perspective*. New York: Harper & Row.

Pine, K. H., & Mazmanian, M. (2016). Artful and contorted coordinating: The ramifications of imposing formal logics of task jurisdiction on situated practice. *Academy of Management Journal*, 60(2): 720–742.

Polidoro, F., & Theeke, M. (2012). Getting competition down to a science: The effects of technological competition on firms' scientific publications. *Organization Science*, 23(4): 1135–1153.

Post, B., Buchmueller, T., & Ryan, A. M. (2017). Vertical integration of hospitals and physicians: Economic theory and empirical evidence on spending and quality. *Medical Care Research and Review*, 75(4): 399–433.

Pratt, M. G., Rockmann, K. W., & Kaufmann, J. B. (2006). Constructing professional identity: The role of work and identity learning cycles in the customization of identity among medical residents. *Academy of Management Journal*, 49(2): 235–262.

Quartz-Topp, J., Sanne, J. M., & Pöstges, H. (2018). Hybrid practices as a means to implement quality improvement: A comparative qualitative study in a Dutch and Swedish hospital. *Health Care Management Review*, 43(2): 148–156.

Raman, R., & Bharadwaj, A. (2012). Power differentials and performative deviation paths in practice transfer: The case of evidence-based medicine. *Organization Science*, 23(6): 1593–1621.

Reay, T., & Hinings, C. R. (2005). The recomposition of an organizational field: Health care in Alberta. *Organization Studies*, 26(3): 351–384.

Reay, T., & Hinings, C. R. (2009). Managing the rivalry of competing institutional logics. *Organization Studies*, 30(6): 629–652.

Reay, T., Golden-Biddle, K., & Germann, K. (2006). Legitimizing a new role: Small wins and microprocesses of change. *Academy of Management Journal*, 49(5): 977–998.

Reay, T., Goodrick, E., & Hinings, B. (2016). Institutionalization and professionalization. In E. Ferlie, K. Montgomery, & A. R. Pedersen (Eds.), *The Oxford Handbook of Health Care Management* (25–44). Oxford: Oxford University Press.

Reay, T., Goodrick, E., Waldorff, S. B., & Casebeer, A. (2017). Getting leopards to change their spots: Co-creating a new professional role identity. *Academy of Management Journal*, 60(3): 1043–1070.

Reay, T., Chreim, S., Golden-Biddle, K., Goodrick, E., Williams, B. E., Casebeer, A., Pablo, A., & Hinings, C. R. (2013). Transforming new ideas into practice: An activity based perspective on the institutionalization of practices. *Journal of Management Studies*, 50(6): 963–990.

Rogers, E. M. (2003). *Diffusion of Innovations* (5th ed.). New York: Simon & Schuster.

Rovik, K. A. (2011). From fashion to virus: An alternative theory of organizations' handling of management ideas. *Organization Studies*, 32(5): 631–654.

Schwalbe, M. L., & Mason-Schrock, D. (1996). Identity work as group process. *Advances in Group Processes*, 13 (113): 47.

Scott, W. R. (2008). Lords of the dance: Professionals as institutional agents. *Organization Studies*, 29(2): 219–238.

Scott, W. R. (2014). *Institutions and Organizations: Ideas, Interests and Identities* (4th ed.). Los Angeles, CA: SAGE Publications.

Scott, W. R., & Black, B. L. (1985). Introduction: Organization theory and mental health systems. *American Behavioral Scientist*, 28(5): 583–586.

Scott, W. R., Ruef, M., Mendel, P. J., & Caronna, C. A. (2000). *Institutional Change and Healthcare Organizations: From Professional Dominance to Managed Care*. Chicago: University of Chicago Press.

Selznick, P. (1949). *TVA and the Grass Roots: A Study in the Sociology of Formal Organization*. Berkeley, CA: University of California Press.

Singh, J., & Jayanti, R. K. (2013). When institutional work backfires: Organizational control of professional work in the pharmaceutical industry. *Journal of Management Studies*, 50(5): 900–929.

Smets, M., Aristidou, A., & Whittington, R. (2017). Towards a practice-driven institutionalism. In R. Greenwood, C. Oliver, T. B. Lawrence, & R. E. Meyer (Eds.), *The SAGE Handbook of Organizational Institutionalism* (2nd ed.) (365–391). London: Sage.

Stryker, S. (2007). Identity theory and personality theory: Mutual relevance. *Journal of Personality*, 75(6): 1083–1102.

Stryker, S., & Serpe, R. T. (1982). Commitment, identity salience, and role behavior: Theory and research example. In W. Ickes & E. S. Knowles (Eds.), *Personality, Roles, and Social Behavior* (199–218). New York: Springer.

Tajfel, H., & Turner, J. (1985). The social identity theory of intergroup behavior. In S. Worchel and W. G. Austin (Eds.), *Psychology of Intergroup Relations* (2nd ed.) (7–24). Chicago: Nelson-Hall.

Tasselli, S. (2015). Social networks and inter-professional knowledge transfer: The case of healthcare professionals. *Organization Studies*, 36(7): 841–872.

Thornton, P. H., & Ocasio, W. (1999). Institutional logics and the historical contingency of power in organizations: Executive succession in the higher education publishing industry, 1958–1990. *American Journal of Sociology*, 105(3): 801–843.

Tucker, A. L., Singer, S. J., Hayes, J. E., & Falwell, A. (2008). Front-line staff perspectives on opportunities for improving the safety and efficiency of hospital work systems. *Health Services Research*, 43(5 pt 2): 1807–1829.

Vakili, K., & McGahan, A. M. (2016). Health care's grand challenge: Stimulating basic science on diseases that primarily afflict the poor. *Academy of Management Journal*, 59(6): 1917–1939.

Valente, T. W., & Pitts, S. R. (2017). An appraisal of social network theory and analysis as applied to public health: Challenges and opportunities. *Annual Review of Public Health*, 38(1): 103–118.

Van Grinsven, M., Sturdy, A., & Heusinkveld, S. (2020). Identities in translation: Management concepts as means and outcomes of identity work. *Organization Studies*, 41(6): 873–897.

Van Offenbeek, M., Sorge, A., & Knip, M. (2009). Enacting fit in work organization and occupational structure design: The case of intermediary occupations in a Dutch hospital. *Organization Studies*, 30(10): 1083–1114.

Villani, E., Greco, L., & Phillips, N. (2017). Understanding value creation in public-private partnerships: A comparative case study. *Journal of Management Studies*, 54(6): 876–905.

Visser, L. M., Bleijenbergh, I. L., Benschop, Y. W. M., & van Riel, A. C. R. (2018). Prying eyes: A dramaturgical approach to professional surveillance. *Journal of Management Studies*, 55(4): 703–727.

Vogus, T. J., & Sutcliffe, K. M. (2012). Organizational mindfulness and mindful organizing: A reconciliation and path forward. *Academy of Management Learning & Education*, 11(4): 722–735.

Wang, M. S., Raynard, M., & Greenwood, R. (2020). From grace to violence: Stigmatizing the medical profession in China. *Academy of Management Journal*. https://doi.org/10.5465/amj.2018.0715.

Westphal, J. D., Gulati, R., & Shortell, S. M. (1997). Customization or conformity? An institutional and network perspective on the content and consequences of TQM adoption. *Administrative Science Quarterly*, 42(2): 366–394.

Wiedner, R., & Mantere, S. (2019). Cutting the cord: Mutual respect, organizational autonomy, and independence in organizational separation processes. *Administrative Science Quarterly*, 64(3): 659–693.

Wilhelm, H., Bullinger, B., & Chromik, J. (2020). White coats at the coalface: The standardizing work of professionals at the frontline. *Organization Studies*, 41(8): 1169–1200.

Wilkesmann, U., Wilkesmann, M., & Virgillito, A. (2009). The absence of cooperation is not necessarily defection: Structural and motivational constraints of knowledge transfer in a social dilemma situation. *Organization Studies*, 30(10): 1141–1164.

Williamson, O. E. (1975). Markets and hierarchies: Analysis and antitrust implications – A study in the economics of internal organization. University of Illinois at Urbana-Champaign's Academy for Entrepreneurial Leadership Historical Research Reference in Entrepreneurship. https://ssrn.com/abstract=1496220.

Williamson, O. E. (1985). Reflections on the new institutional economics. *Zeitschrift für die gesamte Staatswissenschaft / Journal of Institutional and Theoretical Economics*, 141(1): 187–195.

Wright, A. L., Zammuto, R. F., & Liesch, P. W. (2017). Maintaining the values of a profession: Institutional work and moral emotions in the emergency department. *Academy of Management Journal*, 60(1): 200–237.

Yeager, V. A., Zhang, Y., & Diana, M. L. (2015). Analyzing determinants of hospitals' accountable care organizations participation: A resource dependency theory perspective. *Medical Care Research and Review*, 72(6): 687–706.

Yeager, V. A., Menachemi, N., Savage, G. T., Ginter, P. M., Sen, B. P., & Beitsch, L. M. (2014). Using resource dependency theory to measure the environment in health care organizational studies: A systematic review of the literature. *Health Care Management Review*, 39(1): 50–65.

Zietsma, C., Toubiana, M., Voronov, M., & Roberts, A. (2019). *Emotions in Organization Theory*. Cambridge: Cambridge University Press.

Zinn, J. S., Mor, V., Intrator, O., Feng, Z., Angelelli, J., & Davis, J. A. (2003). The impact of the prospective payment system for skilled nursing facilities on therapy service provision: A transaction cost approach. *Health Services Research*, 38(6 Pt 1): 1467–1485.

Cambridge Elements ☰

Organization Theory

Nelson Phillips
Imperial College London

Nelson Phillips is the Abu Dhabi Chamber Professor of Strategy and Innovation at Imperial College London. His research interests include organization theory, technology strategy, innovation, and entrepreneurship, often studied from an institutional theory perspective.

Royston Greenwood
University of Alberta

Royston Greenwood is the Telus Professor of Strategic Management at the University of Alberta, a Visiting Professor at the University of Cambridge, and a Visiting Professor at the University of Edinburgh. His research interests include organizational change and professional misconduct.

About the Series
Organization theory covers many different approaches to understanding organizations. Its focus is on what constitutes the how and why of organizations and organizing, bringing understanding of organizations in a holistic way. The purpose of Elements in Organization Theory is to systematize and contribute to our understanding of organizations.

Cambridge Elements $\equiv$

Organization Theory

Elements in the Series

Comprehending the Incomprehensible: Organization Theory and Child Sexual Abuse in Organizations
Donald Palmer and Valerie Feldman

Starting Points: Intellectual and Institutional Foundations of Organization Theory
Bob Hinings and Renate E. Meyer

Stakeholder Theory: Concepts and Strategies
R. Edward Freeman, Jeffery S. Harrison and Stelios Zyglidopoulos

Re-engaging with Sustainability in the Anthropocene Era: An Institutional Approach
Andrew J. Hoffman and P. Devereaux Jennings

Cultural Entrepreneurship: A New Agenda for the Study of Entrepreneurial Processes and Possibilities
Michael Lounsbury and Mary Ann Glynn

Emotions in Organization Theory
Charlene Zietsma, Madeline Toubiana, Maxim Voronov and Anna Roberts

Professional Occupations and Organizations
Daniel Muzio, Sundeep Aulakh and Ian Kirkpatrick

The Search for the Virtuous Corporation
Justin O'Brien

Organizational Learning from Performance Feedback: A Behavioral Perspective on Multiple Goals
Pino G. Audia and Henrich R. Greve

Healthcare Research and Organization Theory
Trish Reay, Elizabeth Goodrick, and Thomas D'Aunno

A full series listing is available at: www.cambridge.org/EORT

Printed in the United States
by Baker & Taylor Publisher Services